BREAKAWAY

HEART

GARY A. PIAZZA

www.dizzyemupublishing.com

DIZZY EMU PUBLISHING

1714 N McCadden Place, Hollywood, Los Angeles 90028

www.dizzyemupublishing.com

Breakaway Heart

Gary A. Piazza

ISBN: 9781549970184

First published in the United States

in 2017 by Dizzy Emu Publishing

www.dizzyemupublishing.com

Breakaway Heart

By Gary A. Piazza

(based on true events)

WGAW# 1893725

gappman@gmail.com
360-609-7192

FADE IN:

OVER CREDITS - The history of Vietnam as rendered in rich and
colorful silk paintings. Countrysides, pagodas, landscapes,
and daily life blend seamlessly via meticulous brush strokes.

                              DISSOLVE TO:

INT. UC IRVINE - HALLWAY - EVENING

Two professionally dressed VIETNAMESE WOMEN march down a
darkened hallway. They are former refugee and TED guest
speaker, MY LE NGUYEN (Pron. Me Lay Win), and a much younger
Vietnamese intern and TED event coordinator, SHARON VU. My Le
wears a classy skirt and low heels. Her hair and makeup are
spot on. She's in her early forties, but looks much younger.

They stop at a stage entrance, face each other.

                    SHARON
          This is it. How are you feeling?

                    MY LE
          A bit nervous.

                    SHARON
          The audience likes you, remember
          that...and don't forget to breathe.

My Le taps the headset mic with her finger.

                    SHARON (CONT'D)
          Mic is on, you look beautiful.
          You've got this in three, two,
          one...

My Le nods, takes a deep breath, then heads for the stage.

INT. UC IRVINE AUDITORIUM - DAY

The TED stage is empty except for a single round carpet. A
monitor hangs behind the stage, displays a picture My Le.

My Le enters the auditorium confidently. She approaches the
carpet, steps into the light.

The audience claps.

                    MY LE
          Thank you. Many of you know of or
          have heard of the Vietnam war.
                    (MORE)

                              MY LE (CONT'D)
                 You may have even heard the terms
                 'refugee' and 'boat people.' What
                 you might not know is the struggle
                 that took place after 1975 and
                 ended around 1996. A struggle that
                 I was a part of...a struggle that
                 brought me before you today. I'm
                 one of the lucky ones. Of the more
                 than one million refugees who fled
                 Vietnam during that time,
                 approximately thirty percent were
                 killed or lost trying to find
                 happiness abroad. I'm a boat
                 person, and my story may shock
                 you...but that is not my purpose
                 today. Rather, I want to share with
                 you a piece of that twenty-one year
                 exodus and how the bonds of family
                 taught me a valuable lesson about
                 survival and compassion. As a
                 mother and a teacher, I am pleased
                 to tell you and your children what
                 the history books don't. This is my
                 story, my piece of that history,
                 and there are many, many more like
                 it.
                      (beat)
                 I invite you now to take a journey
                 with me...back to a day when my
                 life changed forever...

EXT. VIETNAM - JUNGLE - DAY

Greenery as far as the eye can see. A fully developed
tropical forest. There is brief serenity.

BOOM! A mortar EXPLODES. The scene erupts with the SOUND of
WAR. A firefight ensues. The peaceful jungle becomes a noisy
arena interspersed with VIETCONG AND AMERICAN SOLDIERS.

An American soldier, SERGEANT HATHAWAY, pulls in behind a
tree and takes out his radio. Bullets ricochet.

                              HATHAWAY
                 We're surrounded goddammit! Fire
                 mission, do you read?!

No response.

                              HATHAWAY (CONT'D)
                 Shit!...Fire mission! Do you copy?!

He stows the radio and signals another platoon member,
PRIVATE MAIR, to advance.

Hathaway stands, lays out a cover spray with his M16. The
rounds pierce through the forest.

Mair rushes over, staying low, dodging fire.

>   HATHAWAY (CONT'D)
>   Radio's dead!

>   MAIR
>   So are we if you don't think of
>   something!

>   HATHAWAY
>   Give me the map!

Mair pulls out a well-used map, unfolds it. He sees the town
"My Tho" printed near their location.

>   HATHAWAY (CONT'D)
>   Shit! One way through...

>   MAIR
>   Pull the squad into town!?

>   HATHAWAY
>   Damn right, private! It's improvise
>   or die out here! Now fall back with
>   the squad and prepare to move!

The entire squad of men move out on Hathaway's signal.

The squad becomes overwhelmed. The fight continues as it
approaches town.

EXT. MY THO CITY - MY LE'S GRANDMOTHER'S HOUSE - DAY

SUPER - "MY THO CITY - TET 1968"

Rushing out of the house, EIGHT YEAR-OLD MY LE, in pony
tails, olive pants and open foot sandals, grabs her bicycle.

Her mother, LAN, storms out of the house. She's young, but
war-torn and tired. She stands at porch's edge, watches My Le
ride away.

>   LAN
>   (subtitled)
>   My Le, don't be long!

ON MY LE

She rides through the small village. A few of her NEIGHBORS wave as she passes by.

EXT. MY THO CENTRAL MARKET - DAY

My Le leans her bike against a post.

The market is booming with people and is decorated with New Year fluff. The market stalls extend out into the distance and come to a stop near the Mekong river. Boats along the water's edge make up a floating market.

She walks amongst the produce and fruit stands, passes by stalls with dried sea creatures and boat propellers.

AT NOODLE STAND - RIVER'S EDGE

My Le approaches a noodle stand. The elderly and wrinkled OWNER is busy arranging his stand.

He looks up, sees My Le standing there. Surprised, he pulls the hand-rolled cigarette from his mouth.

                    OWNER
               (subtitled)
          My Le. I was beginning to think you
          left the country.

                    MY LE
               (subtitled)
          We have little money for food. It's
          very difficult right now.

My Le looks over the dried noodle selection.

                    OWNER
               (subtitled)
          You came alone this time. Where's
          your mother?

                    MY LE
               (subtitled)
          Making supper with grandmother.

                    OWNER
               (subtitled)
          Staying in for the festival, eh? I
          don't blame her. Hard to be happy
          with the war going on.

She picks up a bundle of dried rice noodle, inspects it.

                         MY LE
                      (subtitled)
                Same price?

                         OWNER
                      (subtitled)
                Are you kidding? I raise the price
                and you'll never come back!

She forces a small smile as she digs into her purse.

                         OWNER (CONT'D)
                      (subtitled)
                Any sign of your father?

She is silent for a moment then hands him some change. He
takes it, but realizes he's brought up a touchy subject.

                         MY LE
                      (subtitled)
                Not yet.

She grabs the bundle, turns, walks back to her bicycle.

                         OWNER
                      (subtitled)
                We'll be seeing you, My Le!

ON MY LE - STREETS OF MY THO

She enters her neighborhood and is confronted with PEOPLE
running from their houses, SCREAMING, panicking.

Confused, she continues on.

The RATTA TATTA TAT sound of gunfire suddenly shocks her into
reality. She pedals faster.

                         MY LE
                      (don't shoot in Viet)
                Dung ban, dung ban!

She nears her house, she sees the American soldiers in a
firefight with the Vietcong.

Bits and pieces of festival decorations drift into the air.

The moment lingers, her CRIES become washed out by the sounds
of GUNFIRE.

My Le's mother runs down the street barefoot. She sees My Le
approaching on the bike, frantically waives her away.

                         MY LE (CONT'D)
              Maaa! Dung ban!

My Le starts to wobble on the bike and falls over.

She looks up, the SLOW MOTION bombardment of soldier fighting
soldier overwhelms her.

The NOISY arena begins to FADE. We hear only a HEARTBEAT.

Private Mair rears back with a grenade and begins to throw. A
bullet clips his shoulder as he releases the grenade.

The grenade falls short of its target and EXPLODES near Lan.

Lan disappears in the explosion. My Le SCREAMS SILENTLY.

The HEARTBEAT stops.

                         MY LE (CONT'D)
              Maaa! Maaaaa!

Tangled in the bike, she cries herself into shock.

The silence is replaced with DISTORTED AMBIANCE. The gunfire
stops. The last bullet ricochets. The smoke clears.

Sergeant Hathaway walks up to My Le, kneels beside her.
Shocked and stoic, she looks deep into his eyes.

Hathaway can only return a regretful, silent glare.

                                             FADE OUT:

FADE IN:

INT. MY LE'S GRANDMOTHER'S HOUSE - DAY

My Le lies in bed, sick, withered, depressed. Her
grandmother, XUAN, approaches with a cup of water. She's a
long-time survivalist whose body and posture show the pain of
war. She sits down at her bedside. Xuan is careful to display
no emotion.

                         XUAN
                      (subtitled)
              Drink this, small one.

My Le sits up, holds the cup, hands frail. She takes a sip.

She says nothing, just a dry, exhausted look as she settles
back into the pillow.

                         XUAN (CONT'D)
                    (subtitled)
               Your sickness won't leave your body
               until you let go...

She points to My Le's head.

                         XUAN (CONT'D)
                    (subtitled)
               Don't become weak up here!

There is a MORPHING of languages, a TRANSITION from
VIETNAMESE TO ENGLISH.

                         MY LE
               The Americans should die! They are
               bad!

Xuan puts a comforting hand on My Le's forehead.

                         XUAN
               The Americans are not bad.

                         MY LE
               They are. They didn't have to come
               here.

                         XUAN
               Your father was a soldier himself.
               A soldier fighting this very
               war...*with* the Americans.

                         MY LE
               And he's dead, too!

                         XUAN
               You don't know that.

                         MY LE
               Then why won't he come back?

She kisses My Le's forehead and walks into the kitchen.

My Le watches her grandmother as she tends to various kitchen
tasks, cleaning, arranging, etc.

                         MY LE (CONT'D)
               Grandma.

                         XUAN
               Quiet over there. Rest.

                         MY LE
               I need to know if he's still alive.

                    XUAN
          Rest first. Talk later.

                    MY LE
          Please tell me what you know.
          Please. I can't rest until you do.

Xuan returns, sits next to her on the bed.

                    XUAN
          He worked at the embassy for some
          time, then the Americans recruited
          him for some special
          operation...that was two years ago.
                 (beat)
          That's all I know.

My Le simply rolls over and takes comfort with the bedding.
Her eyes display the pain within.

                    MY LE
          I remember him. I see him in my
          dreams...smoking his cigarettes,
          arguing with mom...fishing...the
          sand and ocean...we were a family.

My Le begins to sob.

                    XUAN
          We are still a family.
                 (beat)
          Your father is a strong man and he
          loves you very much. I know he
          would much rather be here with you
          now. Give it some time. The war is
          not over.

INT. SCHOOLHOUSE - DAY

SUPER - "1972"

My Le is twelve now. She sits at a dilapidated wooden desk
amongst her CLASSMATES and listens to a lecture from her
elderly teacher and former farmer, MR. PHAM.

The school bell RINGS. My Le rushes out of the school house.

OUTSIDE SCHOOL

My Le is confronted by a few CLASSMATES.

                    CLASSMATE ONE
          Where are you going, My Le?

                         MY LE
                 To the Library.

                         CLASSMATE ONE
                 Why don't you come with us?

                         MY LE
                 I have to study.

The classmates share a laugh. CLASSMATE ONE looks at My Le's
books. She snatches them from her grasp.

                         CLASSMATE ONE
                 What is this?

She reads the covers and shares with the others. They laugh
at her.

                         CLASSMATE ONE (CONT'D)
                 English? Why do you need that?

                         CLASSMATE TWO
                 Maybe her daddy is an American and
                 she can't understand him!

                         CLASSMATE ONE
                 And this one, "Survival Skills and
                 Tactics."

The classmates laugh. Continue to taunt.

My Le snatches the books back.

                         MY LE
                 Back off!

My Le walks away. The others watch curiously.

EXT. MY LE'S GRANDMOTHER'S HOUSE - EVENING

A full moon hangs majestically over the house.

My Le stands before a healthy papaya tree in the far corner
of the back yard.

She holds her survival book in one hand and practices some
martial arts moves pictured within its pages.

Hanging from one of the branches is a dilapidated hand-made
frame with a fading picture of her father. She kicks and
spins and comes face to face with the photo.

                         MY LE
                    (whispering)
              Come back, papa.

Xuan walks out with two bowls, takes a seat at a small table.

                         XUAN
              Time to eat, small one. Bring me
              the papaya so I can cut them up.

My Le breaks her trance then picks two of the fruit.

My Le sets the papaya and book on the table and takes a seat.
Xuan begins cutting.

My Le has already begun piling food into her mouth.

                         XUAN (CONT'D)
              Slow down, try to taste it first.
              Are you listening?

                         MY LE
              You always told me, "A hungry belly
              has no ears."

                         XUAN
              Sometimes I really worry about you.

                         MY LE
              You said it wasn't healthy to
              worry.

                         XUAN
                    (regarding the book)
              So much your father...in more ways
              than one. You read and practice...I
              just hope you don't need it.

                         MY LE
                    (beat)
              Grandma, why am I different?

                         XUAN
              Different?

                         MY LE
              I get teased. I have no friends.

                         XUAN
              You have no brothers or sisters,
              and that is rare in this country.
              Kids just don't understand the
              virtues of being an only child.

                    MY LE
          Virtues?

                    XUAN
          Benefits. Good things. You have an
          inner strength they desire. You are
          a free spirit, independent, and
          they hate that.

                    MY LE
          Why no brothers or sisters for me?

                    XUAN
          Your parents wanted a big
          family...but it wasn't in God's
          plan.

My Le stops eating, looks into her grandmother's eyes.

                    MY LE
          I wonder if God even has a plan.

INT. SCHOOLHOUSE - DAY

SUPER - "APRIL 30TH, 1975 - THE FALL OF SAIGON"

Fifteen year-old My Le sits in class. Mr. Pham, goes over
Vietnam history.

                    PHAM
          ...My Tho was under Cambodian rule
          until around the seventeenth
          century. After that time, the
          Nguyen Lords...

Mr. Pham is interrupted by the sound of VIETCONG storming the
hallways.

The students are startled.

                    PHAM
          Don't be afraid. Stay seated
          please.

Some students stand and move to the back of the room.

Two VIETCONG soldiers enter the room. A higher ranking
OFFICER follows behind.

                    OFFICER
          The school is closed. Everyone out.
               (to his soldiers)
               (MORE)

                         OFFICER (CONT'D)
          Burn it.

EXT. SCHOOLHOUSE

The class has gathered outside. The school begins to burn.
The students watch horrified.

Mr. Pham has words with the soldiers.

The two soldiers then bind his hands and take him away.

                         MY LE
          Wait! Where are you taking him?

The soldiers raise their guns, point them at My Le.

Mr. Pham turns and shakes his head no.

The officer approaches her.

                         OFFICER
          He's an enemy combatant. You wish
          to join him?

My Le grimaces.

                         OFFICER (CONT'D)
          Go home, all of you, while you
          still have homes to go to.

Pham bows his head as he's taken away.

The students cry as their school becomes a raging inferno.

EXT. MY LE'S GRANDMOTHER'S HOUSE - DAY

PEOPLE litter the street, they carry what they can from place
to place. THE FALL has caused chaos is everywhere.

My Le approaches the house, she is met by her NEIGHBOR, ANH
TRAN, pre-teen daughter of MR. AND MRS. TRAN.

                         ANH
          Hi, My Le. Not to worry you but my
          papa took your grandmother to the
          hospital.

                         MY LE
          Hospital? Why?

                         ANH
          Her chest hurt...

My Le runs into the house, puts her things down, rushes back
outside. She hops on her scooter and tears away.

INT. HOSPITAL - LOBBY - DAY

My Le bolts inside the lobby. MR. TRAN, her well-dressed
middle class neighbor, stops her at the reception counter.

                    MR. TRAN
          My Le, it's okay! She wasn't
          feeling well so she asked me to
          bring her in.

                    MY LE
          Where is she?

                    MR. TRAN
          Resting. They gave her some
          medication to relax her.

                    MY LE
          I want to see her.

                    MR. TRAN
          I don't think...

My Le tears away, approaches the reception counter. She
addresses the NURSE.

                    MY LE
          Where is my grandmother? I need to
          see her.

                    NURSE
          Calm down...tell me her name.

Mr. Tran approaches the counter.

                    MR. TRAN
          She's with me.

                    NURSE
          I see. Mrs. Nguyen is fine
          now...resting. You can go in, but
          don't disturb the others.

                    MR. TRAN
          Left hallway. I'll stay here.

INT. HOSPITAL ROOM

My Le walks into the populated hospital room. Her grandmother lies in a bed at the other end of the room, asleep.

My Le quietly approaches. A single tear drops from her cheek.

At bedside, she stares at the many lines and wrinkles painted on her grandmother's face. She grabs her hand and holds it.

Xuan awakens. She focuses on the face staring back at her.

>   XUAN
>   Small One?

>   MY LE
>   You're okay.

>   XUAN
>   You shouldn't have come, child.
>   It's only gas.

My Le fights the urge to giggle.

>   MY LE
>   Can't fool me, grandmother.

>   XUAN
>   They are going to release me back
>   into the wild tomorrow.

>   MY LE
>   You have to slow down, or you're
>   going to work yourself to death
>   taking care of me.

Xuan begins caressing My Le's hand.

>   XUAN
>   Then I will die a happy woman...

My Le leans over, gives her grandmother a tearful hug.

>   MY LE
>   Grandmother, I need to talk to you
>   about the Vietcong.

>   XUAN
>   I've been told. Saigon has fallen.
>   It's only a matter of time before
>   they've taken everything and put us
>   in reeducation camps.

                    MY LE
          What can we do?

                    XUAN
          You must leave.

                    MY LE
          Me? What about you?

                    XUAN
          I'm afraid not, child.

                    MY LE
          You're all I have. It's just us.

                    XUAN
          I'm too old and broken to make the
          trip, you know this.

                    MY LE
          I'm staying then. I will be taking
          care of *you* now.

                    XUAN
          So much your mother...

                    MY LE
          When you are well enough to leave,
          I will take you somewhere special.

EXT. BEACH - SUNSET

My Le stands at water's edge. The light ocean breeze streams
through her hair.

She picks up a conch shell, begins prying on it. It breaks
apart and cuts into her palm. She quickly drops the shell.

In the surf, her blood swirls and dilutes.

She clenches her teeth, and presses as hard as she can on the
wound. She's forces out the pain.

Xuan approaches, places her feet next to My Le's.

                    MY LE
          Do you remember coming here with
          mother and father?

                    XUAN
          I'll never forget. We couldn't get
          you off the beach.

                    MY LE
          I like to imagine each grain of
          sand is a person in a much larger
          universe. But in this universe,
          there is no war, no hunger, no
          separation. Everyone is happy. The
          beach is life.

They both ponder, looking out over the water.

                    XUAN
          Small one?

                    MY LE
          Yes?

                    XUAN
          I don't want to call you small one
          any longer.

                    MY LE
          I don't mind.

                    XUAN
          You are a woman now. I want to call
          you granddaughter.

Xuan reaches over and grabs My Le's hand, she holds it
tightly, lovingly.

EXT. STREETS OF MY THO - NIGHT

SUPER - "1978"

A tropical storm has the village immured by rain and wind.

My Le runs down the street, food and supplies in one hand,
hat in the other.

INT. MY LE'S GRANDMOTHER'S HOUSE

My Le rushes into the house, slams the door behind, sets the
supplies down, tosses her hat.

                    MY LE
          Grandmother? The storm is here,
          time to pull the geese in.

No answer from Xuan. My Le walks through the house, wiping
her rain-soaked hair from her face.

                              MY LE (CONT'D)
                    Grandmother?

My Le looks out of the back door. She sees the geese bathing
in puddles of rainwater.

OUTSIDE HOUSE

My Le rushes outside and corrals the geese into a small,
wooden hut. She latches the door.

INSIDE HOUSE

She walks through the house, now more soaked than ever.

                              MY LE (CONT'D)
                    Grandmother?

BEDROOM

                              MY LE (CONT'D)
                    Grandmother, the geese are in now.

She stands at the doorway and wipes her wet hair away.

She approaches the bed. She gives her grandmother a light
shake.

                              MY LE (CONT'D)
                    Grandm...

She shakes again. Nothing happens. The body remains prone.

                              MY LE (CONT'D)
                    Grandmother!

She sits down on the bed, begins to weep.

She pulls the blanket back to reveal her grandmother's body.

There is a parchment neatly rolled and protruding out of her
right hand.

My Le pulls it out, unrolls it.

                              XUAN (V.O.)
                    My dearest My Le. I'm so very tired
                    and my body has reached its end. I
                    can feel my soul breaking away from
                    this shell, and I'm hoping this nap
                    is my last--may you find me
                    peacefully asleep.
                              (MORE)

                        XUAN (V.O.) (CONT'D)
                Your father would be proud of you
                and should you ever reunite with
                him, I hope you will bury any pain
                hiding in that heavy heart of
                yours.

She cries over the letter, tears dropping one by one over the
smearing ink.

                        XUAN (V.O. CONT'D)
                I have left you with enough money
                to get you started. Under my bed
                sits a small wooden chest given to
                me by my father...

My Le pulls a woolen blanket up, revealing the chest.

                        XUAN (V.O. CONT'D)
                ...inside is your ticket to
                freedom.

She raises the lid. Inside is a bundle of tightly wrapped
rice paper.

She pulls the rice paper out and begins unfolding it. Nestled
inside are several foil-thin taels of gold.

                        XUAN (V.O. CONT'D)
                Handle it wisely, granddaughter,
                there are many who would harm you
                for it.

She holds the shimmering gold tael up to the candle light.

She places the gold down and resumes with the letter.

                        XUAN (V.O. CONT'D)
                Thank you for taking care of me
                when I needed it most. You're a
                guardian angel with your mother's
                generous spirit. Just remember,
                there is more to life than
                suffering...there is you. Love me
                always, Grandmother.

My Le collapses over the small chest. Her cries, once washed
out by the storm outside, now seem to overpower it.

OUTSIDE HOUSE

My Le fights the storm. She carries the small chest to the
papaya tree.

She finds a spot underneath and begins digging.

She places the small chest in the hole and covers it back up.

She stares at the small scar in the earth and prays.

Above her, the framed picture of her father swings to near
breaking point. She grabs it and pulls the picture out of the
frame. She kisses the picture then stows it.

                              FADE OUT:

FADE IN:

EXT. MY THO CITY - DAY

SUPER - "ONE WEEK LATER"

My Le sits beside the water's edge. Behind her, the dying
remains of the My Tho market.

A DIRTY MAN, dressed in seafarer's garb, approaches My Le.

                    MAN
          You have the money?

                    MY LE
          I have it.

                    MAN
          Give me half now. The other half
          you will give to the captain's
          associate at the dock.

My Le pulls out a thin sheet of rice paper, hands it to the
man.

The man inspects it. Satisfied, he refolds it and places it
under his hat. He gives her a sour sneer then leaves.

EXT. DOCK - NIGHT

My Le approaches a small gathering of PEOPLE. There are about
thirty or forty people standing next to a small junk.

                    CAPTAIN
          The fee is stated by the Captain.
          Hand over your offerings.

Commotion as the people relinquish their gold to the
CAPTAIN'S ASSISTANT.

My Le hands the assistant her gold. The assistant stops her
before she has a chance to board.

                    ASSISTANT
          Wait! Where is the rest?

                    MY LE
          I paid half to your man at the
          market yesterday.

                    ASSISTANT
          Man, what man?

The captain shakes his head no to the assistant.

                    ASSISTANT (CONT'D)
          Nice try.

                    MY LE
          I paid! You have to take me!

The assistant shoves My Le back. She falls to the ground.

The assistant unties the mooring line and pushes off. He
laughs at My Le.

                    ASSISTANT
          Sorry, not this time.

The junk moves away.

                    MY LE
          Come back! I can pay you more!

She sees the sad, disparate faces of the refugees as the junk
blends in with the night fog.

My Le dives into the water. She swims toward the junk.

The captain of the junk throttles up, speeds away.

A PATROL BOAT approaches. Nearly runs her over. A bullet
enters the water next to her head.

The boat moves close to her. TWO PATROLMEN reach into the
water and pull her aboard. They throw her to the deck.

ON DECK

                    PATROLMAN ONE
          Trying to escape? What is your
          name?!

Me Le remains silent. They kick her.

                    PATROLMAN TWO
          Answer the question!

They yank her up off the deck, patrolman one smacks her across the face.

                    PATROLMAN ONE
          Your name!

My Le kicks patrolman one in the groin. He recoils.

Patrolman two uses the butt of his gun to knock her out.

INT. JAIL - DAY

My Le sits in a cell full to the brim with TWENTY INMATES. The floor is dirt, there is a bucket for a toilet. She sleeps.

The INMATES awaken, an OFFICER kicks a bowls of water and stale rice into the center of the floor.

The inmates come alive, groping over the water, reaching for the chunks of rice. My Le remains.

INT. MILITARY OFFICE - MORNING

Morning sun radiates a solid rift of heat through bamboo shades. It's sweltering, humid, the flies are everywhere.

A VC SOLDIER thrusts her into the room. She falls to her knees before a higher ranking, power-hungry OFFICER, PHONG PHAT.

                    SOLDIER
          She will not speak. She has no
          identity. She was carrying only
          this.

He holds up a soggy knapsack-like bag.

                    PHONG
          Empty it.

The soldier opens it and pulls out some wet food. Disgusted, he lets the food fall to the floor.

He pulls out a picture. It is of My Le and her family. He places it on Phong's desk.

Phong takes a long look at the photo, disregards it, tosses it to the floor before My Le.

Phong removes himself from the comfort of his chair. He approaches My Le with a makeshift pointer in his right hand.

My Le remains hunched over on her knees. Hides her head.

                    PHONG
              (using the pointer)
          Look at me.

My Le slowly raises her head.

                    PHONG (CONT'D)
          What is your name?

My Le remains silent, sullen, withdrawn.

Phong taps the pointer forcibly on the top of her head.

                    PHONG (CONT'D)
          Your name!

Shocked and scared, My Le stammers but manages a firm reply.

                    MY LE
          My Le Nguyen.

                    PHONG
          Is that your family in the picture?

                    MY LE
          Yes.

                    PHONG
          They fled and left you behind?

                    MY LE
          No, they are gone...dead.

Phong chuckles.

                    PHONG
          I don't believe you.

                    MY LE
          The war has taken my family. I am
          the last.

Phong paces.

                    PHONG
          How do I know you're not lying and
          they're waiting for you at another
          dock...ready to sail away to
          paradise?

Phong tucks the pointer under his arm, kneels before her and
lifts her chin up with his free hand.

She is repulsed by him and his imposing hot breath.

                    PHONG (CONT'D)
          You will help our cause and you
          will be proud to do it. That is
          your life now.

Phong stands and retreats to the comfort of his desk.

                    PHONG (CONT'D)
          You'll work the plantation and make
          yourself useful. Your refusal will
          result in a sentence far more
          brutal than incarceration in my
          prison.

He leans forward in his chair, smacks the pointer on the desk
forcibly.

                    PHONG (CONT'D)
          Do you understand!?

My Le manages a slow nod. She reaches for the wet picture.

                    PHONG (CONT'D)
          Take her away.

EXT. VIETNAM - RICE FIELD - DAY

My Le is hunched over, picking rice, placing it in satchels.

ARMED SOLDIERS patrol the workforce.

A SHIRTLESS FARMHAND with more gums than teeth approaches
with an ox and cart. He stops next to My Le.

                    FARMHAND
          Load up.

My Le carries her load to the cart, tosses them inside.

The farmhand stops her as she passes back by. He grabs her by
the arm, whispers into her ear.

                    FARMHAND (CONT'D)
          I might be able to help you out.

                    MY LE
          Let go of my arm.

                    FARMHAND
          I can help you escape.

                    MY LE
          I don't need your help.

She tears away from his grasp.

                    FARMHAND
          Look at you. You won't last here
          and you certainly won't make it out
          on your own.

                    MY LE
          I will manage.

He moves her out of view of one of the soldiers.

                    FARMHAND
          Do you want to be like them? Spend
          the rest of your life here?

                    MY LE
          Why do you care?

                    FARMHAND
          I am well liked, I could get you
          special privileges here. I can help
          you escape...that is if you're
          willing to help me out too.

                    MY LE
          Help you?

                    FARMHAND
          One night. That's all. I'm a lonely
          man.

Aggravated, she pushes him in the chest. He falls into the
mucky water and stirs up a noticeable splash.

TWO GUARDS take notice and rush over to the cart.

The man gets up and stands embarrassed, angered, and wet.

                    GUARD ONE
          Why aren't you working?

                    FARMHAND
          I slipped and fell.

My Le returns to the job at hand.

INT. HUT - NIGHT

My Le lies in her bed, staring at the thatch roof above.

There is a RUSTLING SOUND outside the hut.

My Le gets out of her bunk. She gathers her shoes and puts them on. She places her pillow under the blanket and disappears into the darkness.

The farmhand pokes his head inside the hut.

Under the moonlight, the farmhand slowly creeps inside.

He approaches My Le's bunk, pulls the blanket back and sees the pillow.

Out of the darkness, My Le runs across the room and kicks him into the bamboo wall.

OUTSIDE HUT

My Le runs from the hut and into the dark jungle.

The farmhand stands at the doorway, holding his head, SCREAMING of her escape.

                    FARMHAND
          Guard! She's escaping! Guard! There
          is an escape!

EXT. JUNGLE - NIGHT

My Le runs as fast as she can into the darkened jungle. The jungle opens up for her. She continues well beyond the farm.

She stops near a large tree, catches her breath. Exhausted, she sits against the tree and passes out.

                            DISSOLVE TO:

EXT. JUNGLE - MORNING

My Le awakens, rubs her face, looks up at the arm-like limbs which seem to reach out to her.

She brushes the debris from her clothing and smacks at the bugs crawling on her arms and neck.

There is a smoky blanket of stagnant air present. She sniffs, looks in the direction of the source, begins to walk.

ENCAMPMENT - MORNING

She approaches a campfire, cautiously squats next to it.

There is a CLICK. A gun barrel is placed into her neck.

>   MAN
>   Turn around. Slow.

My Le turns slowly. The gun remains on her head.

She sees a dirty VIETNAMESE MAN with very few teeth, a long grey beard, and a soldier's cap. He stinks of filth.

>   MY LE
>   I mean no harm. I'm just warming
>   myself.

>   MAN
>   Where did you come from?

>   MY LE
>   A plantation nearby.

>   MAN
>   Which plantation? There are many.

>   MY LE
>   Hom Kieu.

The man lowers the rifle. He smiles.

>   MAN
>   Congratulations.

>   MY LE
>   Huh?

>   MAN
>   You have traveled far. You are safe
>   now.

The man gathers some of the wood around the fire and throws it on top.

>   MAN (CONT'D)
>   They won't come for you here. You
>   are young and they are lazy.

>   MY LE
>   What is your name?

The man squats down next to the fire.

>   MAN
>   Oh, no, no, no, no. No names.

                              MY LE
                    I understand.
                         (beat)
                    You have been here a while?

                              MAN
                    A while...probably. But who knows?

The man stands and faces My Le.

                              MAN (CONT'D)
                    Would you like some food?

                              MY LE
                    Thank you. But I prefer to take
                    something with me.

                              MAN
                    I see. Stay here.

He walks bow-legged and semi-hunched over toward his bedding.

He returns with a wadded up shirt.

He presents it to her, opens it, inside is an old compass, a
few pairs of dog tags, a match holder, a few pieces of
jewelry and some face paint.

                              MAN (CONT'D)
                    Where are you headed?

                              MY LE
                    My Tho City.

                              MAN
                    Take this.

He pulls the dilapidated compass and a plastic match holder
out of the wadded up shirt.

She takes the compass and matches.

                              MAN (CONT'D)
                    My Tho is southeast, I believe.
                    Stay low in the brush, and watch
                    out for roving patrols near the
                    farms.

                              MY LE
                    I will, thank you. What about the
                    food?

                              MAN
                    Food...yes.

The man walks over to his bedding and returns a moment later
with a handful of bundled leaves and a small canteen of
water.

>   MAN (CONT'D)
>   Rice. Unfold it and eat it. The
>   water won't last long so sip it.
>   You're very close so you shouldn't
>   need too much food.

>   MY LE
>   Thank you, sir.

>   MAN
>   Will you be staying long?

>   MY LE
>   I know I have troubled you, but I
>   need to keep moving.

>   MAN
>   Your eyes tell me you have a great
>   passion for what lies beyond those
>   trees.

My Le nods, looks at the compass, then at the jungle before
her.

>   MY LE
>   Thank you.

She begins walking.

INT. CAVE - NIGHT

There is a RUSTLING of bushes, the CRUNCH of a light step. My
Le approaches the cave entrance.

She strikes a match and pokes her head inside.

Striking another match, she lights a twig. It ignites and
soon she has a camp fire.

She opens the canteen and takes a small drink. She sits back
against the cave wall and takes off her shoe.

She pulls out the wrinkled picture of her family and stares
at it under the glow of the campfire. She presses the picture
to her forehead and closes her eyes.

>   DISSOLVE TO:

INT. BEACH - DAY - FLASHBACK

She is six or seven and My Le stands at water's edge with her
father. He throws a baited fishing line into the water, hands
her the line.

Her mother and grandmother sit in the sand behind them,
peeling lychee fruit.

                    MY LE
          Papa, I got a fish! I got a fish!

                    NAM
          Pull it in slow...here, let me help
          you.

They work together to land the creature. It turns out to be a
crab.

                    NAM
          Wow, he's a big one.

                    MY LE
          Yummy! I love crab!

Nam tosses the crab to Xuan and Lan, smiles, then re-baits My
Le's hook.

He hands her the crude line and she tosses into the water.

The moment SLOWS, the sound of My Le laughing, giggling and
having fun with her father intensifies then...

                                        CUT TO:

INT. CAVE - MORNING

...the THROATY CAWING sound of an unseen jungle creature.

My Le awakens, rubs her eyes, looks at the dead campfire.

She pulls out her canteen and searches for one last drop of
water.

She finds her family picture on the ground, looks at it
briefly then puts it in her pack.

EXT. JUNGLE - MORNING

My Le EXITS the cave and begins walking into the jungle.

EXT. MY THO OUTSKIRTS - CEMETERY - DAY

An ancient cemetery, crowded with decaying headstones. The
faded epitaphs are barely readable.

Covered in bug bites and exhausted, she approaches quietly.

She walks deep into the cemetery and stops before two
headstones. They bear the name of Xuan, her grandmother and
Lan, her mother.

She kneels before the headstones. She lowers herself, the
headstones RISE INTO VIEW.

She pulls out her family picture.

Weeping now, she places it between the two headstones.

                    MY LE
          Please forgive me for what I'm
          about to do, but I will not give up
          until I have found papa. I love you
          both.

My Le bows her head and remains put.

INT. TRAN HOUSE - EVENING

The TRAN FAMILY, a middle-class ensemble of four, sit quietly
in the living room. Their living conditions and clothing
after the fall show no signs of prosperity.

There is a KNOCK at the door.

MR. TRAN gestures for Anh, his daughter, to answer. Her
younger brother, LINH, reads a book.

MRS. TRAN and Anh walk to the door. Anh opens. There stands
My Le, dirty, tired.

                    ANH
          My Le!

Anh and Mrs. Tran greet her at the door.

MRS. TRAN pulls My Le into the house like a worried mother.

                    MRS. TRAN
          Oh, my! My Le, you're ragged. Anh,
          make a spot for My Le.

                    MR. TRAN
          She can have my spot.

They escort her in and set her down on Mr. Tran's favorite chair.

TRAN HOUSE - KITCHEN

My Le sits at the table in fresh clothes. She tells the family her story over a fresh bowl of pho.

                    MY LE
          I need to find my father.

                    MRS. TRAN
          Not a good idea.

                    MR. TRAN
          There is danger everywhere.

                    MY LE
          I'm not afraid.

Mr. Tran stands and paces the kitchen.

                    MRS. TRAN
          Papa...you know better. She's safer
          here with us.

                    MR. TRAN
          Safer, but not at all content.

                    MRS. TRAN
          Papa...

                    MR. TRAN
          Your father may be in America.

                    MY LE
          How do you know?

                    MR. TRAN
          We found this in your grandmother's
          mail not long after she passed. I'm
          afraid there was no return address.

He hands her a letter. She opens it. Reads it quickly.

                    MY LE
          He's safe in a camp...but that is
          all. It only says he's trying to
          convince the UNHCF to send him to
          America.

                    MR. TRAN
          He could be anywhere by now.

My Le shoves the bowl aside, stands up.

>   MY LE
>   Then you must help me!

>   MRS. TRAN
>   Papa...

>   MR. TRAN
>   (beat)
>   I know some...people. They are good
>   people. There is a boat leaving in
>   three days but...

>   MY LE
>   But what?

>   MRS. TRAN
>   Papa...you know this is wrong.

Mr. Tran sits back down and faces My Le.

>   MR. TRAN
>   Quiet, mama!
>   (beat)
>   At least we can help her make it to
>   the right boat this time.

My Le grabs Mrs. Tran's hand, kneels before her. Their eyes
meet.

>   MRS. TRAN
>   She will need gold. We don't have
>   that much to spare.

>   MY LE
>   I have some, but not enough.

>   MR. TRAN
>   I will make room for you on that
>   boat. I hope God forgives us for
>   what we're about to do.

>   MY LE
>   Thank you. I will not forget your
>   generosity, nor will God.

EXT. MY LE'S GRANDMOTHER'S HOUSE - MORNING

My Le stands before the Papaya tree. The morning sun pokes
through its branches, tickles her hair.

She kneels and begins digging frantically with her bare hands. Soon the top of the chest becomes visible.

She picks it up out of the hole, brushes the dirt away. She stares at it for a moment before prying the lid open.

The last tael of gold. She removes it, presses it firmly on her lips, closes her eyes.

> MY LE
> Thank you, grandmother.

She turns to walk away but sees one papaya hanging near her. She picks it, smells it, stows it in her bag.

INT. BUS - SUNSET

My Le sits in a crowded bus full of Vietnamese WORKERS. She has fresh clothes, a fresh face, but tries to hide her fear.

> MR. TRAN(V.O.)
> Take the commuter bus out of My Tho
> to Den To. Outside of Den To, there
> is a road called Ba Mui Oi road.
> Take it all the way to Tram Xang...

She stares out of the window, daydreams.

TIME TRANSITION - In and out of the bus as it covers the landscape, making stops, letting off passengers.

INSIDE BUS - ON MY LE

My Le looks down the aisle of the bus and out of the windshield as it comes to the last stop.

EXT. TRAM XANG - NIGHT

My Le steps out with a small pack strapped to her back. The driver closes the door and speeds off.

> MR. TRAN(V.O. CONT'D)
> Once in Tram Xang, walk about one
> kilometer to the water...

My Le hikes down the dark road. Behind her a couple of lights from the small town.

> MR. TRAN(V.O. CONT'D)
> Stay near the road but keep an eye
> out for patrols. Before you know
> it, you will be at the river.
> (MORE)

                         MR. TRAN(V.O. CONT'D) (CONT'D)
               There will be only one boat and a
               small crowd...

AT RIVER'S EDGE

My Le approaches the river's edge cautiously.

Sitting before her, a small junk measuring ten meters.

A gathering of thirty REFUGEES stand near the boat while
others board.

                         MR. TRAN(V.O. CONT'D)
               The boat captain is an old friend.
               He will be expecting you. Good
               luck, My Le, and God bless. We hope
               you reach your father safely.

AT BOAT

My Le approaches cautiously. She doesn't recognize anyone in
the group.

Refugees hold suitcases, belongings, useless items.

The BOAT CAPTAIN and his WIFE, both weathered and wrinkled
from years on the boat. He holds a flashlight, frantically
gives instructions for boarding as his wife takes the
offerings.

                         CAPTAIN
               Board quickly please. Leave all
               large objects behind! There is no
               room for suitcases and luggage!

My Le waits in line. In front of her, a WOMAN holds a
sleeping BABY. My Le stares emphatically at the baby.

The Captain rips the bags from some of the refugees, tosses
them aside.

                         CAPTAIN (CONT'D)
               No room for this on the boat! Keep
               moving, that's it, come on...

My Le approaches the Captain's wife.

She hands her the offering.

                         CAPTAIN'S WIFE
               You must be My Le?

                         MY LE
               I am.

                    CAPTAIN'S WIFE
          Tran said you would come alone. You
          can be part of our family for now.

The wife takes the offering and stacks it in her hand with
the others.

                    MY LE
          Thank you.

                    CAPTAIN
          She is the last?

                    CAPTAIN'S WIFE
          She is.

ON BOAT

The boat, or junk, is a converted and hollowed-out fishing
boat. It has a small console or helm and a less than spacious
deck and semi-open bilge.

My Le boards and squeezes in near the back.

The captain starts the motor and puts the boat in motion.

                    MY LE (V.O. PRESENT)
          I was now officially a refugee, and
          like many before me, my fate rested
          in the hands of strangers and the
          foreboding waters.

The evening moon glow shimmers over calm waters as the boat
departs.

                    MY LE (V.O. PRESENT CONT'D)
          I had heard the stories of what
          lies ahead in the South China
          Sea...but I had no idea it would be
          so bad.

                                        FADE OUT:

FADE IN:

EXT. OCEAN - DAY

SUPER - "DAY ONE"

The ocean is massive, uninviting. My Le hangs her head over
the edge of the boat and vomits.

My Le is pale, sweaty, tired. She lets an arm dangle in the
water then wipes her mouth clean.

She glances across the cramped boat. Everyone is sick.

She takes a small rice paper-wrapped lemon half out of her pack. She sticks it in her mouth and sucks the juice from its core.

Next to her, a YOUNG WOMAN nurses an eight month-old BABY, their eyes meet.

>   MY LE
>   What is your child's name?

>   TRAN
>   Liem. After his grandfather.

>   MY LE
>   Liem. I like that name.

A MAN near My Le stands and pees over the side of the rocking boat. He nearly falls overboard.

>   MY LE (CONT'D)
>   I am My Le.

>   TRAN
>   Tran.

>   MY LE
>   You have a beautiful baby, Tran.

>   TRAN
>   Thank you.

>   MY LE
>   His father is not with you?

>   TRAN
>   He had to leave before us. He waits
>   now at a camp in Galang.

>   MY LE
>   I'm sure he can't wait see you
>   both.

>   TRAN
>   It's been six months and we haven't
>   heard from him. We can only hope at
>   this point.
>   (beat)
>   I'm feeling very ill right now, My
>   Le. I'm sorry, but I need to rest.

Tran leans back against the boat and cradles her son. She falls fast asleep.

My Le stares into the faces of mother and child.

The Captain's Wife stands at the bow, makes an announcement to the group.

> CAPTAIN'S WIFE
> The boat does not have a toilet. We
> ask that the women come to the bow
> to relieve themselves. We have a
> large blanket for privacy.

EXT. OCEAN - DAY

SUPER - "DAY THREE"

It's scorchingly humid. Black clouds above cast a late afternoon darkness over the water.

The boat motors slowly through light ocean swells. Everyone is sick, hungry, parched.

INSIDE BOAT

My Le walks between the huddled group. She makes her way toward the captain's helm.

There is a barrel between the helm and the bow. She approaches the captain.

> MY LE
> May I have some water please?

> CAPTAIN
> Can you hold out?

> MY LE
> I have held out more than the
> others. You know this.

The captain takes a small cup and dips it deep into the barrel. He hands her the cup.

My Le drinks the paltry serving of water and hands him the cup. We see that she does not swallow all of the water.

BACK OF BOAT

My Le sits in her spot next Tran.

Tran tries to breast feed but she's unable. Liem is crying.

My Le takes a hardened rice lump and places it in her hand. She spits the water onto the rice, forms it with her hands.

                    MY LE
          Here, give this to Liem.

She hands Tran the softened rice ball. Tran Feeds Liem.

                    TRAN
          How old are you, My Le?

                    MY LE
          Eighteen.

                    TRAN
          Try not to look eighteen out here.

She nods then pulls the papaya out of her pack. She tries to
hide it, showing only Tran.

                    MY LE
          Take this for yourself. Eat what
          you can.

                    TRAN
          Where did you get it?

                    MY LE
          I grew it.

                    TRAN
          I can't, it's yours and...

                    MY LE
          Eat it. Leave nothing behind. You
          need to provide for Liem.

Tran takes the papaya, bites into it. They eat in secrecy.

                    TRAN
          Thank you. That was kind of you.

There is a quiet exchange of appreciation as they eat.

                    MY LE
          I think our captain is lost.

                    TRAN
          I have wondered myself.

                    MY LE
          He had the look of worry.

                    TRAN
          We must pray then.

My Le gazes back down over the deck. She sees another REFUGEE dry heaving as he lies half-asleep.

Yet another REFUGEE is curled up in a ball and MANY MORE lie about sick, filthy and anemic.

Tran looks curiously at My Le as she stares into the distance.

                    TRAN (CONT'D)
          You are alone.

                    MY LE
          Yes.

                    TRAN
          You have no family?

                    MY LE
          That's right, how can you tell?

                    TRAN
          You haven't spoken of a single
          family member.

                    MY LE
          It's true, they are gone.

My Le sighs then pulls out her family picture. Shows Tran.

                    TRAN
          That's okay, you don't--

                    MY LE
          --my mother was killed in a
          firefight near my house when I was
          ten. My father disappeared during
          the war with no trace, and I lost
          my grandmother recently to old age.
          I am the last.

                    TRAN
          No brothers or sisters?

                    MY LE
          No. We were a family of only's.

                    TRAN
          I see something else in those
          beautiful eyes of yours...but I
          can't quite place it.

                    MY LE
          I haven't gotten over the loss.
          That is what you see.

Tran nods, remains quiet after that.

EXT. OCEAN - DAY

SUPER - "DAY SIX"

The oceans are unrelenting. Huge swells engulf the boat.

ON BOAT

Refugees hang on for their lives. Water consumes the boat.

The storm grabs the boat, tosses it about. Refugees are
thrown across the deck.

They help each other up, struggle to hold on to whatever they
can.

My Le approaches Tran, fights her way across the slippery
deck.

Tran is holding on for dear life. Liem is not visible.

                    MY LE
          Liem! Where is Liem!?

                    TRAN
          I lost him! Help me! Help me,
          please!

My Le looks frantically around the deck. She sees Liem's
blanket near the edge of the bilge.

She slides across deck and peers into the compartment.

POV - MY LE - Liem floats face down in the watery
compartment.

My Le jumps inside.

INSIDE BILGE

It's cramped and flooded. She sees Liem floating haplessly,
tossing about with each rock of the boat.

She grabs Liem and turns him over quickly.

                    MY LE
          Liem! Liem!

She wipes the water away from his face and opens his mouth.

A wave POUNDS the boat, sending her under water with Liem.

She comes back up and is disoriented, yet she still has Liem.

                    MY LE (CONT'D)
              Please! Please! Liem!

She makes several attempts to resuscitate. The boat continues
to toss.

Liem chokes and coughs to consciousness. Relieved, she kisses
his forehead and cries out her satisfaction.

                    MY LE (CONT'D)
              Yes! Yes! You're alive,
              Liem...breathe! That's
              it...breathe!

Liem belts out a cry.

ON BOAT

My Le pulls herself out of the compartment with one arm. She
has Liem tucked tight with the other.

She stumbles across the pitching deck and meets up with Tran
who is barely conscious.

                    MY LE
              Tran. Wake up. I have Liem. Take
              him. Take him.

She places Liem in Tran's arms, huddles against them both.

The storm continues, the pounding of the ocean continues. We
FADE OUT of the storm and into...

EXT. OCEAN - DAY

...a dead calm.

SUPER - "DAY EIGHT"

The humidity and blistering sun consume the boat.

ON BOAT - PORT SIDE

There is commotion near the side of the boat.

The captain helps an older MAN. He clutches the dead body of
his WIFE.

The man will not let go, he insists on holding her limp body.

> CAPTAIN
> You must let her go. She is gone.

> MAN
> N...noo...sh...sh, she stays w-with
> me. Please God, please God...

The captain pries the man's hands from his wife. He rests her body against the gunwale of the boat.

The captain asks a YOUNGER MAN close by for help.

> CAPTAIN
> You look well. Give me a hand with
> her.

The young man approaches the woman's body.

Once again, the husband clutches her body, groping, clinging.

> CAPTAIN (CONT'D)
> Sir, let go. She's gone.

> MAN
> Please God, please God!

The Captain pushes the man away. The Captain and young man wrap the woman in a blanket.

They both lift, slowly raising the body to the edge of the boat.

OUTSIDE BOAT- WATER LEVEL

The woman's body is lowered slowly into the water. Her husband tries to prevent the burial, but finally succumbs, collapsing in exhaustion.

INSIDE BOAT

> TRAN
> I knew them. They lived near me.

> MY LE
> I'm sorry.

> TRAN
> They have been together more than
> twenty years. I am sorry, too.
> (beat)
> (MORE)

>   TRAN (CONT'D)
>   I've been praying, My Le, but it
>   looks as if we'll be joining her
>   soon.

My Le's eyes are locked on the event port side.

The reflection of a dying boat becomes apparent in each
pupil. We CLOSE IN further and TRANSITION to another day.

EXT. OCEAN - DAWN

A blanket of white morning fog drifts over the ocean. The
calm water is eerily SILENT.

SUPER - "DAY NINE - THE RAID"

A boat MOTOR becomes audible. The boat trolls INTO FRAME.

My Le opens her eyes, sees the boat moments before it RAMS
the refugee boat. Bodies fly, people scream.

The boat, comprised of a eight THAI CREW (PIRATES) wearing
sarongs, hold swords and AK-47's.

Startled, My Le begins rubbing dirt, vomit, feces, all over
her face and arms. She does the same for Tran while trying to
shake her awake.

>   MY LE
>   Tran, Tran! Wake up, wake up! We
>   have to cover our bodies. They
>   won't touch us if we're filthy.

Tran is out, barely responsive.

>   TRAN
>   Where is Liem?

>   MY LE
>   He's here. He's here, just hold
>   him. Come on, Tran. We're being
>   boarded. You need to help me!

>   TRAN
>   (groggy)
>   I...can't...take care of Liem. Take
>   him to his father...

My Le shakes her as she trails off.

>   MY LE
>   Tran. Tran!

The pirates are positioned at all corners of the boat,
watching, smoking...scanning eagerly. Pure evil incarnate.

The DRIVER powers down the motor and lets the boat drift.

Three THAI PIRATES rush to the bow.

They pull the refugee boat close and tie up.

The men and their driver stand fast with guns.

                    DRIVER
                (subtitled Thai)
            Fresh meat.

The driver walks through the filth on the decaying vessel,
peering down at the dismal faces of the refugees.

The captain peers up and sees the man standing before him.

The driver stares at the blisters and bumps on the captain's
unshaven face.

                    CAPTAIN
                (delirious)
            You have come to help us?

The driver laughs and turns away from the captain. He
whistles at his crew to join.

The three men jump onto the refugee boat and approach the
driver.

                    DRIVER
                (subtitled Thai)
            They still have their belongings.
            Take it all. Throw the dying over
            then bring the men forward and
            strip them down.

My Le sits and hides her face between her knees.

The pirates begin searching. They rip the only belongings
from the weakened refugees. There is crying, screaming.

The pirates come across a body of an OLDER MAN. They give him
a kick, but he only moves a little.

They pick him up and throw him over.

The women who remain alive sob their last bit of energy away.

My Le reaches into her small pack and pulls out two small
balls of hardened rice and a dried lemon peel.

She stuffs it all into her mouth and swallows.

Tran is barely coherent. Liem cries as he slowly falls out of her arms.

My Le grabs the baby from her arms and holds it tight against her chest. Tran's body slumps, limp, ragged, lifeless.

                    MY LE
          Tran!

My Le cups her mouth to hold back a cry.

FRONT OF BOAT

The driver fires his gun into the water barrel. It is empty.

He grabs the captain up off his console and turns him around face down. He places the rifle in the back of his head.

                    DRIVER
               (subtitled Thai)
          Gold?

The Captain can only moan.

                    DRIVER (CONT'D)
               (subtitled Thai)
          Last chance...

Still no response.

The driver lowers the gun and fires it into the captain's right leg.

He collapses to the deck.

The captain's wife SCREAMS and throws herself at the driver.

The driver points the gun at her and fires. She falls dead in front of her husband.

Grief-stricken, the captain submits.

                    CAPTAIN
          G-g-gold. We have...g-g-gold.

The driver relaxes his grip on the gun, smiles.

The captain uses his last bit of energy to reach out for the gun and swing at the driver. He misses.

The driver pushes the captain to the deck, steps on his
wounded leg. He puts the gun to the captain's head. Spares
him.

All hell breaks loose. The pirates tear up the boat, ripping
the belongings from the refugees, firing their guns into the
engine bay.

The pirates gather the men together and stand them in a row.
They have stripped them of their clothes.

The driver approaches the first refugee.

                    DRIVER
               (subtitled Thai)
          Open your mouth.

He inspects then moves on to the next refugee.

                    DRIVER
               (subtitled Thai)
          Open...

The driver signals one of the pirates to hold the refugee's
hands tight.

The driver uses a pair of pliers to pull out a gold tooth.
The refugee struggles, blood pours from his mouth.

My Le cowers back with Liem in her arms. She watches
helplessly as the process repeats itself.

Tran is shaken by the Bow Man but doesn't respond.

She is taken from the deck by the Bow Man and thrown
overboard.

My Le begins to tremble uncontrollably as Tran's face slowly
disappears over the edge of the boat.

The Bow Man grabs My Le by the arm and stands her up. He
shakes his head.

                    BOW MAN
               (subtitled Thai)
          We'll just have to hose you down,
          make you pretty again.

                    MY LE
          Don't hurt my baby...please!

The Bow Man takes the baby from My Le. He cradles it in his
arms teasingly.

                              BOW MAN
                         (subtitled Thai)
                    Tiny baby. He is not yours though.

He grabs My Le by the arm and escorts her across the deck.

He approaches pirate two.

                              BOW MAN (CONT'D)
                         (subtitled Thai)
                    I won't be long with her.

                              PIRATE TWO
                         (subtitled Thai)
                    I'm next, right?

                              BOW MAN
                         (subtitled Thai)
                    Looks like there's enough to go
                    around. Call the others on the
                    radio.

ON PIRATE BOAT

The Bow Man pushes her onto the boat. She stands there,
frightened, shivering.

Pirate two begins hosing her down, washing the filth away. My
Le covers her face. He slaps her hands away, sprays her face,
wipes away more dirt.

He shoves her toward the steering console. Through the center
is a stairwell into the boat.

                              BOW MAN
                         (subtitled Thai)
                    Inside.

INSIDE SLEEPING QUARTERS

The Bow Man pushes My Le into the small room. She stands
there as he places the child on an opposite bunk.

My Le presses her lips together.

The Bow Man pulls a crude wooden door shut on the stair
entrance. The room becomes as dark as My Le's situation.

ON REFUGEE BOAT

The group of pirates pull the rings and jewelry off the dead
and dying. They pocket everything of value no matter how
small. More crying and struggling.

OUTSIDE BOAT

A second THAI FISHING BOAT approaches. Seven or eight more
PIRATES board the two boats.

There is a reunion of sorts, a pass-down of information
between pirates. The new pirates are eager, hungry, excited.

ON PIRATE BOAT

The LEAD PIRATE from the new boat walks to the lower hold of
the first pirate boat. He bangs on the door.

Outside the door, we hear the sound of Liem crying.

                    LEAD
               (subtitled Thai)
          Save some for us, brother!

INSIDE SLEEPING QUARTERS

We CLOSE IN on Liem as he CRIES amidst the unrelenting
physical exploitation on My Le.

On the bunk wall, a faint shadow of the act, brutal and
without compunction. Liem's CRIES become louder and louder,
blending in with the painful CRIES from all around.

                                        FADE OUT:

FADE IN:

INT. REFUGEE BOAT - MORNING

The boat is in shambles. The pirates have left nothing.

SUPER - "DAY ELEVEN"

My Le lies asleep on the deck of the boat, Liem pressed
close. Her face rests on the dirty planks. A single drop of
rain impacts her cheek, then another, and yet another.

The deluge begins.

My Le removes her torn, rain-soaked shirt, wrings the water
into Liem's mouth.

She gets up and crawls toward the bow of the boat. Many are
holding up bowls, containers, to capture the rain.

She passes by the remaining survivors. Children moan the
words, "mum, mum, mum" indicating they are hungry.

She approaches the water barrel near the bow and stares at it's bullet-ridden shell.

She grabs hold of it and drags it into the rain.

As she peers inside, she sees the sparkling reflection of the gold tael foil resting in its bottom.

She pulls a handful of gold out and stares at it. She rears back as if to throw it overboard.

A hand reaches out and grabs her, stopping the throw.

A MAN, the husband of the first dying woman, stands behind her.

>   MAN
>   Our...gold. Why would you throw it
>   over?

>   MY LE
>   It has no value. It's blood money.

>   MAN
>   Is it blood money if it can save
>   just one of us?

She ponders.

>   MY LE
>   If it is here, it can betray us.

>   MAN
>   You overestimate the intelligence
>   of the pirates. Now leave it in the
>   barrel and let it catch this rain.

She places the gold back inside then drags the barrel to a more open area of the boat.

The rain pours in. It fills the barrel to the first bullet hole and begins to leak out.

She signals the others to take advantage of the trickle.

>   MY LE
>   Water! We have water! Hurry, take
>   all you can!

The remaining refugees get up and grab any and all containers they can muster. They find plastic tarps and spread them out over the surface of the boat.

The barrel spits out the rain water in small, steady streams.

The thirsty savor the taste of the water, pushing, shoving, groping for the clear survival potion.

As time passes, the deluge turns into torrential rainfall. The boat begins to fill up quickly.

> CAPTAIN
> God has given us more than we need, my friends. We have to remove the water or we'll capsize!

The refugees look at him curiously, hesitantly.

> CAPTAIN (CONT'D)
> I know you're all thirsty, but you must do this now or we'll sink! Come on! Move it! Move it!

The refugees begin bailing the water. Many cry as they do so, and many are unable to move at all.

But they are not fast enough. The boat continues to fill.

My Le helps bail water whilst holding Liem with one arm. She pauses and looks up at the sky.

> MY LE
> Please, God, have we not been tested enough? Is this how you will have us die?

There is a BEAT, then the skies relent and the rain subsides. There is relief amongst the refugees.

> DISSOLVE TO:

EXT. OCEAN - DAY

SUPER - "DAY THIRTEEN"

There is commotion. The refugees hear the captain SHOUTING.

They lift their heads, look out over the water and see an island. There are other boats nearby.

My Le walks to the front of the boat, approaches the captain.

> MY LE
> An island?

> CAPTAIN
> Yes, and there are others.

The captain steers the boat toward the island. Two boats near
the shore head toward the refugees.

                    MY LE
          Look, here they come. Oh, thank
          God, they're going to help us!

The remaining refugees approach the bow, there is hope in
their eyes.

The captain presses on, the refugees rejoice.

There is a WHIZZING sound, a ricochet, near My Le's head.
Then another, and yet another. A bullet splinters the helm,
rounds pierce the water.

                    CAPTAIN
          Get down! They're firing at us!

The refugees cover their heads and fall to the deck in near
panic.

The two boats approach, one gets close enough for
communication.

The captain remains at his console, hands in the air. A
Malaysian BOAT OFFICER addresses the refugees.

                    BOAT OFFICER
          You can't dock here. The camp is
          full.

                    CAPTAIN
          We need food...water. We're dying.

                    BOAT OFFICER
          We'll tow you out. You'll have to
          find another island.

My Le approaches the gunwale with Liem in her arms.

                    MY LE
          We need food and water! Please help
          us! There are babies...children.
          They will die soon if you don't
          help!

The boat officer ignores her, turns his back.

My Le hands Liem off to the captain then jumps from her boat
to the patrol boat.

The officers immediately apprehend her.

                         MY LE (CONT'D)
              Heathens! We just need food and
              water! Tow us out if you must, but
              give us something to *eat*!

The boat officer looks deep into her eyes then converses with
his crew.

They toss a few scraps of food and some water over to the
refugee boat.

The refugees scramble to pick up the food and water.

Another CREWMAN ties a line from the Malaysian boat to the
refugee boat.

The boat officer's crew releases My Le and hands her some
additional food and water.

                         BOAT OFFICER
              Keep sailing, there are many
              islands nearby.

My Le holds the supplies in hand and makes her way back to
her boat, retrieves Liem.

The patrolman begin pulling the refugees out to sea.

INT. REFUGEE BOAT - NIGHT

My Le lies on the deck of the boat. Liem sleeps quietly on
her chest. She looks up at the stars, reaches out to them,
twirls her palms.

                         MY LE (V.O. PRESENT)
              The stars above reminded me of the
              endless grains of sand on my
              favorite beach. So far apart from
              one another, yet so close in
              meaning to me. This journey across
              the borders, this "vuot bien" as we
              called it, gave me some quiet
              moments which allowed me to pray
              and to reflect.

My Le strokes Liem's dark baby hair. She kisses his head,
rubs his back.

Night MORPHS into morning. The sunrise casts a golden glow on
the horizon.

                              MY LE (V.O. PRESENT CONT'D)
                    For the others, the journey had
                    taken its toll, only fifteen of the
                    original thirty remained. We were
                    barely alive and had given up
                    hope...but then our luck changed
                    for the better. Was God listening?

EXT. REFUGEE BOAT - MORNING

There is a THUD, the boat is impacted by another. The
refugees are met by TWO VIET MEN.

                              VIET MAN ONE
                    We're here to help! Attach this
                    rope and we'll pull you in!

The refugees come alive. The captain takes the line and
attaches it.

                              CAPTAIN
                    Finally, some friendly faces!

The captain and the others take a deep breath, smiles appear.

My Le stands with Liem in her arms, she approaches the bow
and looks out over the water. An island comes into view.

SUPER - "DAY FIFTEEN - PULAU KUKU, INDONESIA"

EXT. KUKU ISLAND - MORNING

The captain eases off the boat, holds his wounded leg. He
reaches down and grabs a handful of sand.

The two boat men and THREE VIETNAMESE walk up to the
refugees, offer assistance.

                              CAPTAIN
                    Everyone is sick and weak. Please
                    help them off the boat.

The rescuers board, the boat men remain, speak to the
captain.

                              CONG
                    Welcome to Kuku island, I'm Cong
                    and this is my brother, Le. How
                    long were you at sea?

                    CAPTAIN
          I don't know. A couple of weeks at
          least.

                    CONG
          You're safe now. We help each other
          here on the island.

                    CAPTAIN
          We are grateful.

The refugees are helped off the boat. Many are in tears, all
are happy to be on solid ground.

My Le helps herself off the boat with Liem in her arms. She
sees only trees and makeshift huts. She approaches Le.

                    MY LE
          Where is the camp?

                    LE
          You're looking at it. We are
          building it ourselves.

                    MY LE
          Building it? With what?

                    LE
          With our hands, young lady. Now
          follow the others, we have food and
          water in the camp.

My Le walks toward the huts.

                    CAPTAIN
          How many people are here now?

                    CONG
          About one hundred, including your
          group. We get more each day.

                    CAPTAIN
          Thank you. I doubt we could have
          made it another day.

AT CAMP

The camp is crude, with huts made of old boat lumber, plastic
sheeting, tree limbs tarps and palms. Clothes lines run from
huts to trees and a few children play nearby.

The tropical rains begin. The refugees make their way without
noticing. Each is greeted by someone in the camp.

My Le approaches the huts. A WOMAN, mid-twenties, holding a
bamboo hat to her head, runs from her hut.

>   THUY
>   Come, bring the baby out of the
>   rain!

My Le follows her into the hut.

INT. THUY'S HUT

Thuy dips a cup into a water bowl then walks it over to My Le
and Liem.

>   MY LE
>   Thank you.

My Le feeds Liem first. He begins to cough and cry.

My Le cradles him in the other arm, tries again. Again, Liem
cries. My Le becomes frustrated.

>   THUY
>   May I?

My Le hands Liem to Thuy. She refuses. Helps reposition him
on My Le.

>   THUY (CONT'D)
>   No, you hold him, but put him on
>   your shoulder like this. Give him a
>   few pats on the back while rocking
>   him.

My Le looks at Thuy, looks for affirmation. Thuy nods.

>   THUY (CONT'D)
>   You must be hungry.

Thuy stands and hands her a small cup of rice.

My Le devours the rice, scooping it all into her mouth with
her hand.

>   THUY
>   I am Thuy. I am here with my two
>   boys and my husband.

>   MY LE
>   I am My Le. This is Liem.

My Le gazes up at a picture of Thuy and her boys. She looks
confused as there are three boys in the picture.

                    MY LE
          I see three boys...

                    THUY
          We lost one of the boys on our trip
          here.

                    MY LE
          I am sorry.

Thuy refills the cup, hands it to My Le.

                    THUY
          Try giving him the water again.

My Le cradles him in her arm. Thuy assists. Liem is relaxed
and drinking the water.

                    MY LE
          There is much to learn with
          children.

                    THUY
          Indeed, especially when they are
          not yours.

                    MY LE
          How did you know?

                    THUY
          No resemblance...and when I first
          saw you, it wasn't the way you
          carried *yourself*, it was the way
          you carried *him*. Like a pack mule
          carrying its cargo.

My Le looks a bit puzzled, hurt.

                    THUY (CONT'D)
          No, no, no. I don't mean that in a
          bad way. If you are not his mother,
          then you are his savior, and you
          are the most important person in
          his life right now. I could see
          that right away.

                    MY LE
               (beat)
          Pack mule?

They both start giggling.

A MAN enters the hut, Thuy's husband, BINH. He carries a
container of water. Sets it down at one end of the hut.

                         THUY
               My husband, Binh. Binh, this is My
               Le and Liem.

                         BINH
               Your from the group that just
               arrived?

                         MY LE
               Yes.

                         BINH
               Welcome to Kuku. Hopefully it will
               be a short stay. You can rest here
               tonight, but we'll need to build
               you a hut of your own in the
               morning.

                         MY LE
               You are very generous.

                         BINH
               You will need to be just as
               generous when others arrive. We
               take care of each other here on the
               island. We must if we want to
               survive.

My Le nods in agreement.

                         MY LE
               I wish to meet your sons. Where are
               they?

                         BINH
               Out gathering palms and wood for
               the huts. They have more energy
               than you can handle, so be careful
               what you wish for.

                         THUY
               We really need to get you and Liem
               cleaned up and into some cleaner
               clothes. We'll burn those.

My Le pulls her shirt up to smell. She wrinkles her nose.

                         BINH
               I'll show you where you can bathe,
               but only if you feel you have
               enough energy to make the walk.

                    MY LE
          I can do it. I would even crawl on
          my belly to get a bath.

                    THUY
          Liem can stay here if you don't
          mind. I Have water to clean him
          with.

EXT. JUNGLE - DAY

My Le and Binh walk out of the camp and into the jungle. They
don't get far before encountering a tiny cemetery with
makeshift headstones, many bare or without identification.

                    MY LE
          So many...

                    BINH
          Sadly, there will be more. Malaria,
          dehydration, Deng fever...suicide.
          We're all at risk.

They walk out of the cemetery and continue through the
jungle. They arrive at a stream as it cascades out of the
jungle canopy.

                    BINH
          The stream is broken down into
          sections.

UPSTREAM

My Le and Binh approach a small pool attached to the stream.

                    BINH
          Top section. This is where you can
          collect water. The stream brings
          with it a fair amount of germs, so
          you'll need to boil it before
          drinking.

MID-STREAM

My Le and Binh approach the bathing area. There are WOMEN AND
CHILDREN bathing in the stream.

                    BINH
          Middle section. This is for bathing
          only.

DOWN-STREAM

My Le and Binh approach the wash portion. The area is empty.

> BINH
> This is the last section. It's for
> washing clothing mostly...or soiled
> items. It is important that you
> remember how this works.

> MY LE
> I will remember, thank you, Binh.
> If you don't mind, I think I'm
> going to bathe now.

> BINH
> Take your time. The first bath is
> always the best.

EXT. THUY'S HUT - MORNING

My Le stands outside the hut in cleaner clothes, her skin
clean, her hair up. She looks out over the ocean as the sun
climbs on the horizon. She closes her eyes, smells the
breeze.

Binh walks out of the hut, stands beside her, smokes a
cigarette.

> BINH
> Are you ready for this?

> MY LE
> I am.

The boys, ten year-old TOAN and twelve year-old HUNG, race
out of the hut, chasing each other, playing tag, being boys.

> BINH
> Hey, hey! It's not play time. We
> have work to do.

> MY LE
> You were right about the boys. They
> do have a lot of...spirit.

> BINH
> It can be a virtue.

> MY LE
> Ah, yes...virtue. A good thing. A
> very good thing.

                    BINH
          Come on, I have a spot you might
          like.

EXT. MY LE'S CAMP SITE - MORNING (MOMENTS LATER)

SERIES OF SHOTS - My Le and the men building her hut:

- Palms placed in a pile.

- Bamboo placed as poles in each corner.

- Toan and Hung horse around, get smacked by Binh.

- Walls built with boat lumber and tree limbs.

- Walls attached to poles.

- Roof put on as the rain pours.

- Binh, the boys, and My Le admiring their work. Binh smokes.

BACK TO SCENE

My Le hangs a painted sign with her boat number near the
entrance.

                    BINH
          Yours is even better than ours.
          Must be the woman's touch.

                    MY LE
          Thank you so much for the help. I
          couldn't have done it without you
          and the boys.

                    BINH
          You're pretty crafty...good with
          your hands. That will come in handy
          around here.

Binh holds a small bucket. He hands it to My Le.

                    MY LE
          For water?

                    BINH
          No, toilet. It's not always easy to
          run into the jungle when you have
          to go.

INT. MY LE'S HUT - DAY

My Le puts the bucket in the far corner. She arranges a small pile of palms and a blanket as a bed.

She takes her family picture out of her pocket, kisses it, then tucks it on the wall above the bedding. She kneels before it and prays silently.

Thuy walks into My Le's hut with Liem. My Le finishes and greets Thuy.

                    THUY
          He wanted to see his new home.

Thuy hands Liem to My Le.

                    MY LE
          Welcome, little man.

                    THUY
          What will you do with Liem when
          you've reached one of the main
          camps?

                    MY LE
          Do?

                    THUY
          Adopt him? Turn him over to the UN?

                    MY LE
          Before his mother died, she told me
          his father was waiting for them in
          Galang. I will request to be
          transferred there with him when the
          next delegation arrives.

                    THUY
          There have been very few supply
          boats to the island, and even fewer
          representatives. Prepare yourself
          for a long stay.

INT. MY LE'S HUT - NIGHT

My Le awakens to SCREAMS, COMMOTION outside.

She gets up, peers outside, sees people running toward the beach.

She takes a glance over at Liem who is fast asleep, then joins the others.

AT BEACH - NEAR DOCK

She approaches the beach, sees bodies being pulled from the
water. She pauses from shock, then jumps in to help the
others.

She pulls a SMALL CHILD from the water. The child is
unresponsive.

There is SHOUTING, more commotion, as the group continues to
pull bodies from the water.

My Le places the child on the beach, begins to resuscitate.

Binh carries the body of a woman out of the water and places
her next to My Le. He finds no pulse.

                    BINH
          My Le.

My Le ignores Binh, continues to work on the child. Binh
checks for pulse on the child.

                    BINH (CONT'D)
          My Le! I'm sorry. There are more
          and we need your help.

He places a hand on her shoulder, helps her up.

                    MY LE
          We need to save them all...

She looks out over the water, the moonlight casts its silvery
glow over a debris field littered with bodies. She looks up
at the heavens, closes her eyes.

                    MY LE (V.O. PAST)
          Oh, Lord, please give us the
          strength to survive when strength
          is in short supply...

She opens her eyes, heads for the water to bring more bodies
ashore.

                    MY LE (V.O. PAST CONT'D)
          Give us the guidance we need to
          make a clear path to freedom...

She finds the body of a woman and pulls her ashore. Binh
helps her drag the body to the sand. He reaches down to check
the pulse. He shakes his head and heads back for the water.

                         MY LE (V.O. PAST CONT'D)
                    Free us from starvation and
                    sickness and the darkness all
                    around us...

My Le finds a BOY, a teenager. She pulls him ashore, checks
for pulse.

She gives the boy a few breaths then rolls him on his side.
She pats his back and repeats.

                         MY LE (V.O. PAST CONT'D)
                    And give us the breath to fill our
                    dying friends with life.

The boy coughs and sputters. My Le holds him close to her.

                         MY LE
                    You're going to be okay. It's okay.
                    Shhh...

Binh walks up to her and the boy. Kneels beside.

                         BINH
                    We've cleared all the bodies we
                    could find. He seems to be the only
                    survivor, thanks to you.

                         MY LE
                    No thanks to me, Binh. This should
                    not be happening to our people.

                         BINH
                    Young man, what happened out there?

                         BOY
                    We were too far out when we sank
                    the boat.

                         MY LE
                    You sank it?

                         BOY
                    Yes, sir. We didn't want to get
                    towed back out again.

My Le looks out over the water. She closes her eyes once
again as tears roll down her cheeks.

EXT. JUNGLE - CEMETERY - AFTERNOON

My Le follows Binh's family into the cemetery. Incense burns.
TRADITIONAL VIET TUNES are played out with sticks and bowls.

There are makeshift headstones on the newly excavated graves.

My Le stands in semi-circle with the rest of the group. She is silent, withdrawn.

A woman approaches one of the wooden caskets. She begins cutting the buttons off of the deceased.

> MY LE
> What is she doing?

> THUY
> We don't bury the dead with
> buttons. Buttons are bad luck.

An ELDER addresses the dead in Vietnamese, speaking of the final rest, the afterlife, and the ultimate sacrifice.

My Le is transfixed by the headstones. She is taken back to her grandmother's death. In FLASHBACK V.O., she hears her grandmother's words from the goodbye letter.

> XUAN (V.O.)
> "...you're a guardian angel with
> your mother's generous spirit. Just
> remember, there is more to life
> than suffering...there is you."

The ceremony continues. Thuy takes note of My Le's detachment.

> THUY
> You feel guilty...that somehow it
> should be you in that grave.

Thuy leans in, gets close.

> THUY (CONT'D)
> You're a survivor by your own hand,
> My Le. Freedom has a price when the
> heart loses hope.

> MY LE
> But this hurts so much.

> THUY
> Don't let that pain stop you from
> helping our people survive. Your
> father would be proud of the way
> you give your heart and soul to
> others.

> FLASHBACK TO:

EXT. MY LE'S GRANDMOTHER'S HOUSE - DAY

A very young My Le and her father finish digging a hole.

Nam places a papaya tree into the hole. They begin
backfilling with dirt.

> NAM
> The papaya is life, My Le. It will
> feed us when we are hungry. We have
> a saying, "When eating a fruit,
> think of the person who planted the
> tree."

> MY LE
> But I'm hungry now. When can we eat
> it?

> NAM
> Silly, girl. You must first nurture
> it...care for it...help it grow. If
> you do this, it will reward you
> with beautiful fruit.

My Le purses and bows her head. Nam is puzzled.

> NAM (CONT'D)
> Why the sad face? The tree will
> bring happiness to us all.

> MY LE
> I'm not sad, papa.

> NAM
> Then, what is it?

> MY LE
> You did this for us because we're
> poor and hungry.

He lifts her chin, looks into her eyes.

> NAM
> No, child, *we* did this so you can
> learn how to give back.

BACK TO PRESENT - CEMETERY

> MY LE
> Thank you, Thuy, for keeping me
> focused.

                    THUY
          We've all been through harsh times.
          We must all stay focused.

The ceremony has wrapped up. People place flowers, incense,
and candles next to the new graves as they EXIT.

My Le takes a flower and places it next to one of the graves
and leaves with Thuy and her family.

                    MY LE
          You have helped me in so many ways.
          Now I want to help you.

                    THUY
          With what?

                    MY LE
          Would you mind if I teach the boys
          English?

                    THUY
          Was that your area of study?

                    MY LE
          It was. I'm quite good, I think.

                    THUY
          That would be fine with me. Binh?

Binh shrugs, smiles and continues walking with the boys.

INT. THUY'S HUT - MORNING

My Le sits with the boys, Hung and Toan, and works on the
alphabet.

                    MY LE
               (subtitled Vietnamese)
          One more time. Let's start with the
          alphabet again.
               (English)
          A...B...C...D...

The boys catch on, follow, giggle.

My Le joins in to assist and enunciate each letter.

Thuy watches and smiles.

                    MY LE (V.O. PRESENT)
          My time with the boys was even more
          valuable than I had anticipated.
               (MORE)

                    MY LE (V.O. PRESENT) (CONT'D)
          They caught on quickly and it made
          me realize that I had found a
          purpose, a calling, that didn't
          involve dealing with the dead or
          dying. I would teach.

We RISE UP out of the hut and above the encampment.

EXT. KUKU CAMP - TIME TRANSITION - DAY/NIGHT/DAY

The encampment grows, more huts appear, more people populate
the island and mill about, tending to various tasks.

Boats pull in, people get off, huts and structures pop up.

EXT. MY LE'S HUT - DAY

My Le stands before a small group and reads passages from a
book. The class looks on. She's in the moment, enjoying her
makeshift class.

EXT. JUNGLE - DAY

My Le and Thuy collect water from the stream.

                    MY LE (V.O. PRESENT CONT'D)
          I began to settle in, learn how to
          survive, and help others along the
          way.

SERIES OF SHOTS - MY LE ON THE ISLAND

- My Le picks fruit from a tree, places it in a burlap bag.

- My Le and Thuy wash clothes together in the stream.

- My Le and Liem playing together. He's walking.

- She cooks food over an open fire. Brings food to others.

- Unloading UNHCR, CARE, and Feed The Children supplies.

- Helping with construction efforts.

                    MY LE (V.O. PRESENT CONT'D)
          But the island was no picnic, and
          our exodus brought with it many
          shameful atrocities.

EXT. JUNGLE - MORNING

More COMMOTION. The camp comes alive, My Le carries Liem into
the jungle, follows the others. There is a crowd. Everyone is
staring up.

A man hangs from a tree.

                    MY LE (V.O. PRESENT CONT'D)
                He watched as each member of his
                family succumbed to sickness. The
                shame of not being able to help
                them...overwhelming.

EXT. BEACH - DAY

More refugees arrive. The sick, the dying. The dead.

                    MY LE (V.O. PRESENT CONT'D)
                The cycle continued...an endless
                supply of refugees made their way
                to the island. Once there, many
                realized the horror of not knowing
                what lies beyond. We had no home to
                go back to and no country of
                residence. There was death, but no
                toll. We were unclaimed and
                invisible...unwanted.

EXT. HONG KONG HARBOR - DAY

Aerial view of the harbor, clogged with refugee boats.

                    MY LE (V.O. PRESENT CONT'D)
                And there were many refugee camps.
                Hong Kong...

EXT. THAILAND - LAEM SING DISTRICT - DAY

Aerial view of the coast, refugee boats parked ashore.

                    MY LE (V.O. PRESENT CONT'D)
                Thailand...

EXT. MALAYSIA - PULAU BIDONG - DAY

Aerial view of the crowded camp.

                    MY LE (V.O. PRESENT CONT'D)
          Malaysia...

EXT. KUKU ISLAND - DAY

Aerial view of Kuku. Barely a shantytown.

                    MY LE (V.O. PRESENT CONT'D)
          Singapore, Philippines and our very
          own Kuku island in Indonesia. We
          were everywhere, and many of us
          were stuck, left to languish in
          these camps for years.

INT. ADMINISTRATION HUT - DAY

A DELEGATION from the U.S., the Philippines and Malaysia, sit
at a table. My Le sits across, a look of disappointment on
her face.

                    MY LE (V.O. PRESENT CONT'D)
          Delegations came and went. I was
          refused transfer each time, and the
          search for my father continued
          unsuccessfully. Without family or
          connections abroad, my chances of
          leaving Kuku any time soon were
          slim...or so I thought.

INT. MY LE'S HUT - NIGHT

My Le is curled up at one end of the hut. She's sick, sweaty,
breathing is labored, in and out of consciousness.

Liem CRIES loudly, My Le is too sick to attend to him.

Thuy and Binh enter the hut and find My Le barely responsive.

MY LE'S POV - Blurred figures, more CRYING, unintelligible
dialogue, a blanket tossed over her...then BLACKNESS.

INT. INDONESIAN RED CROSS HOSPITAL (PMI) - DAY

SUPER "GALANG REFUGEE CAMP - 1979"

FROM BLACKNESS - A hospital room. Not the neatest. My Le lies
in one of the small beds.

She awakens slowly. Checks her surroundings. More blurriness,
confusion. She's a bit addled, restless.

A NURSE walks in, tries to calm her. Tends to he needs of the room.

                  NURSE
         It's okay. You're safe here.

                  MY LE
         Safe? Where?

                  NURSE
         Pulau Galang. Indonesia.

                  MY LE
         But I...

                  NURSE
         Shh...rest first. Talk later.

The nurse walks out.

                  MY LE
         Where's Liem? Excuse me!

My Le tries to get up but is too weak. She falls back.

                  MY LE
         Where's Liem!!??

There is a brief pause and more frustration, then...

A MAN walks into the room carrying Liem. He approaches My Le.

                  MINH
         I think he misses you.

My Le composes herself, exhales, smiles.

                  MY LE
         He's okay.

                  MINH
         Of course he is. How do you feel?

                  MY LE
         I don't know. I don't know where I
         am...how I got here, or how long
         I've been asleep. The nurse said
         I'm in Galang. Is that true,
         doctor?

                  MINH
         It is true, yes, you've been asleep
         for about two weeks.

Minh steps closer. He stands at bedside.

                    MINH (CONT'D)
          But I'm no doctor. I'm Minh Vu,
          Liem's father.

My Le cups her mouth, begins to tear up.

                    MY LE
                 (muffled)
          I'm sorry, Tran...she fought...

                    MINH
          It's okay, I know what happened. I
          know she didn't make it. I want to
          personally thank you for all you've
          done for my family.

                    MY LE
          But I didn't...

He pulls a letter from his pocket, unfolds it.

                    MINH
          The family who sent you here
          explained it in this letter. It was
          addressed to both of us.

                    MY LE
          Family?

                    MINH
          Binh and Thuy. Your neighbor
          friends on Kuku. They finished this
          letter on the boat and stuffed it
          into your clothes.

He hands her the letter.

                              FLASHBACK TO:

EXT. KUKU ISLAND - NIGHT

SUPER "TWO WEEKS BEFORE"

A large boat sponsored by WORLD VISION sits dock side. It is
the SEASWEEP. A few refugees are allowed to board once they
are verified.

INT. MY LE'S HUT - NIGHT

Binh rushes into the hut, sees Thuy writing a letter. The
boys sit next to an unconscious My Le. Liem lies asleep in
the background.

                        BINH
              Come on, momma! Our name was the
              last to be called. We need to board
              now if we're going to get off this
              island. Finish it later!

Thuy folds up the letter, stuffs it in her pocket.

                        THUY
              Grab Liem and help me with My Le.
              They are going with us.

Binh becomes annoyed.

                        BINH
              No! They won't let us on.

                        THUY
              Help me with them! Boys, come on!

                        BINH
              We can't! The boat has limited
              space and they are not on the list.

Thuy approaches Binh, gets within a nose.

                        THUY
              We're not leaving them here. They
              deserve a chance. Do you hear me?
                  (beat)
              She has saved a life...lives! Now
              it's her turn to be saved. We do
              this, or I'm staying back with the
              boys. I won't take "no" for an
              answer.

The boys are on mom's side, it's written on their faces.

Binh takes a glance around the hut, bites his lip, then nods.

Thuy pushes Binh, he turns then she smacks him on the head.

                        THUY (CONT'D)
              Move your ass, old man! Come on!

EXT. KUKU ISLAND - DOCK - NIGHT

Binh's family approaches the Seasweep gangplank. Binh holds
My Le in his arms.

A BOATSWAIN'S MATE stands by.

                    BOATSWAIN'S MATE
          Family name and number please?

                    BINH
          Nguyen. Number 24150.

The boatswain looks through the manifest.

                    BOATSWAIN'S MATE
          I see four listed but you have six.

                    BINH
          Our friend needs help. Can she
          board with us?

                    BOATSWAIN'S MATE
          Why haven't you had one of our
          people look at her first?

                    THUY
          We thought we could help, but then
          she worsened.

The Boatswain heads up the gangplank and talks to another
CREW MEMBER. Binh's family stays put.

Moments later, the Boatswain returns with the crew member and
the CAPTAIN of the Seasweep.

                    CREWMEMBER
          We'll have our doctors look at her,
          but we can't take the entire group.

                    CAPTAIN
          I'm sorry, folks. We are limited
          and can't do this without splitting
          you up.

                    THUY
          Her child must go with her.

                    CAPTAIN
          We can do that, but have room for
          two more only. Like I said, we'll
          have to split you up, or you can
          wait for the next boat.

                         BINH
                    (subtitled Viet)
          Momma, this is our chance. We don't
          know when the next boat will
          arrive.

                         THUY
                    (subtitled Viet)
          There will be others. We'll be
          fine. I'm not splitting us up. She
          will die here if we don't do this.

                         BINH
                    (subtitled Viet)
          We can die here, too!

                         THUY
                    (subtitled Viet)
          Go then. Take one of the boys with
          you. Go! Go! Go!

                         CAPTAIN
          Ma'am. Ma'am!

More arguing, then a MAN wearing khakis, and a sweaty button
up shirt, walks down the gangplank. He is the World Vision
president, STAN MOONEYHAM.

                         MOONEYHAM
          Folks, why the ruckus?

                         CAPTAIN
          Sir there seems to be some
          confusion as to who is boarding.

                         MOONEYHAM
          I see. And who is to board?

                         CAPTAIN
          This family, but they have a sick
          friend who is not on the list.

Mooneyham looks over the group. Analyzes.

                         MOONEYHAM
          Does that put us over?

                         CAPTAIN
          By two, sir.

                         MOONEYHAM
          Let them board. All of them. And
          get her to the infirmary right
          away.

Big smiles from everyone.

>   THUY
>   Thank you, Mr. Mooneyham. You're a
>   savior.

>   MOONEYHAM
>   God bless you child.

Binh hands My Le over to the crew member.

Thuy kisses Liem's cheek, hands him to the captain.

>   THUY
>   Hope to see you on the other side,
>   little one.

INT. GALANG RED CROSS HOSPITAL ROOM - BACK TO PRESENT

>   MY LE
>   They didn't stay here. It says they
>   went to another camp to rendezvous
>   with other family members.

She tries to get up again and manages. She swings her legs
over the side of the bed.

>   MINH
>   You need to take it slow.

>   MY LE
>   I'm fine. I want to see them.

>   MINH
>   They are at another camp, My Le.

>   MY LE
>   I will go to the other camp.

>   MINH
>   You can't! The other camp is in the
>   Philippines.
>   (beat)
>   You can try to reconnect with them
>   at another time. That is your only
>   option.

Sadness washes over My Le's face.

>   MY LE
>   May I hold Liem?

Minh gently hands Liem over. Color returns to her face. She
rocks him gently.

                    MINH
          There is more, My Le. Liem and I
          will be transferred as well. We
          have a sponsor waiting for us in
          America.

                    MY LE
          But, so soon?

He sits next to her and Liem on the bed.

                    MINH
          My volunteer work here has opened
          some doors for me. I will try to
          help you off the island as well.
          It's the least I can do.

                    MY LE
          I'm more interested in finding my
          father. Can you help me?

                    MINH
          I'll do what I can. For now you
          will remain in camp one.

                    MY LE
          Camp one?

                    MINH
          There are three camps here on
          Galang. One is for new inductees.
          Camp two is for those transferring
          soon. The accommodations are a bit
          nicer there. Camp three is the
          cemetery. You are pretty good with
          English I hear, so I've arranged to
          have you help one of my volunteer
          friends in camp one. You'll like
          him, his name is Gaylord.

She nods, forces a smile.

                    MY LE
          When do you leave?

                    MINH
          Next week.

                    MY LE
          Then I would like to spend as much
          time with Liem as I can.

                         MINH
                 We would like that.

EXT. GALANG CAMP - RESETTLEMENT PROCESSING CENTER - DAY

My Le carries a handful of supplies out of the office. She
reads the camp directions with her free hand.

GALANG CAMP - BETWEEN BUILDINGS AND PATHS

My Le gets a good look at the camp. She passes by a makeshift
coffee hut, a store hut, and the school hut. She observes
life in the camp and its occupants. KIDS play, ADULTS trade
items and mill about, conversing, smoking, relaxing.

EXT. GALANG CAMP - REFUGEE BARRACKS

My Le approaches the long, two-story structure. She checks
her map, compares the building number on the barracks.

She enters the building.

INT. BARRACKS

My Le walks in, finds an empty bunk near the opposite end of
the building. She takes a seat, checks her surroundings,
looks at OTHERS as they mind their own business.

In walk Minh and Liem.

                         MINH
                 It's a lot better than the sand at
                 Kuku, but not as private.

                         MY LE
                 It's a blessing to me.

                         MINH
                 Have you had a chance to walk
                 around the camp? Check things out?

                         MY LE
                 Yes. It's much bigger than Kuku.

                         MINH
                 If you get a chance, climb up the
                 hill and visit the Mahayana temple.
                 It's quite a view and good for
                 prayer.

                    MY LE
          I will do that. Maybe I'll take
          Liem and we can pray together.

                    MINH
          Good. Once you get settled in here,
          meet me at building six. We'll have
          some food ready for you there.

INT. BUILDING SIX - EVENING

My Le, Minh and Liem sit on the floor. A low-rise table
covers the length of the room. REFUGEES sit and drink tea and
eat.

                    MY LE
          You have more family waiting for
          you?

                    MINH
          Yes, in the America. My brother and
          his wife are helping with my
          sponsorship.

                    MY LE
               (beat)
          Tell me about Tran, your wife. If
          you don't mind.

                    MINH
          I worked for her father in a rice
          mill near Saigon. He immediately
          took a liking to me. Our families
          were very similar and we shared the
          same values. I remember seeing her
          on occasion. She would come by the
          rice mill where I worked, and each
          time she did, I fell in love all
          over again.

My Le giggles.

                    MINH (CONT'D)
          It's true, and her father noticed
          my reaction each time she walked
          into the office. We connected
          eventually, and she told me she had
          the same crush on me. The rest is
          history. We married, had Liem, and
          the country died before our eyes.
               (beat)
          I'll never forget the smile on her
          face when Liem was born.

                    MY LE
          I am sorry, Minh. She was a brave
          woman. She gave her own life to
          keep Liem alive.

Minh holds up his tin tea cup.

                    MINH
          And so have you. Cheers.

INT. PRIMARY/SECONDARY SCHOOL HUT - MORNING

My Le walks into the hut carrying two lychee fruit. She is
the only one present.

A MAN walks in, thin and tall, bearded, carrying a happy and
pleasant demeanor. He introduces himself to My Le.

                    BARR
          Hello there. You must be My Le.

                    MY LE
          Yes.

                    BARR
          Gaylord Barr. I'm one of the
          volunteers here. They said you'd be
          helping me.

My Le holds out the lychee fruit.

                    MY LE
          For you, teacher.

Barr holds up his hands as if to stop her.

                    BARR
          Oh, no, no, no. You keep those. I
          have something for you instead.

He holds up a papaya fruit.

                    BARR (CONT'D)
          You can eat it, or use it to trade
          up to something bigger in the camp.

My Le takes the papaya and admires it.

                    MY LE
          My favorite, thank you.
               (beat)
          Will you teach English only?

                    BARR
          Some English, some math. I'm really
          here to help around the camp.
          Teaching's only part of it...

Barr sees My Le holding the papaya up to her nose. She's
drifted off in thought.

                    BARR (CONT'D)
          Look, My Le, I know the trip was
          rough. I know what happens out
          there on the water. If you're not
          up for this...

                    MY LE
          No, no. It's fine. I was thinking
          of my father. I miss him.

                    BARR
          I'm sorry.

She pulls out the wrinkled picture and hands it to Barr.

                    MY LE
          Still alive. Somewhere in America I
          believe. I gave his information to
          the UNHCR, but they have no record.
          Can you help me?

                    BARR
          I'll see what I can do. Okay?

She offers a soft smile.

EXT. GALANG CAMP - CHUA KIM QUANG TEMPLE - MORNING

An orange sunrise blankets the sky. The temple glows.

My Le passes by two lion statues, pulls her rucksack off. She
takes a seat with Liem on the temple steps.

                    MY LE (V.O. PAST)
          Our last day together. I'm going to
          miss this little man.

Liem crawls around on the steps, plays with a small pebble.

                    MY LE (V.O. PAST CONT'D)
          You have your reasons for bringing
          us together Lord...perhaps that
          part of _my_ quest has been
          fulfilled.

PEOPLE pass by, mostly elderly, smile at My Le and Liem.

> MY LE (V.O. PAST CONT'D)
> If that is so, then please give him
> a chance at a good life.

My Le picks up Liem and walks toward the temple.

She kneels at a shrine near the entrance. Liem sits beside.

> MY LE (V.O. PAST CONT'D)
> If you can find it in your plan to
> reunite us someday, that would be a
> true blessing. Thank you, Lord...

ON MY LE - She finishes the prayer, hands folded, speaks...

> MY LE
> Amen.

EXT. CAMP STORE - LATER

My Le approaches a shanty store with Liem in hand.

THREE YOUNG GIRLS sell cigarettes, canned milk, coffee and
tissue among other items.

One of the girls plays with a Polaroid camera, snaps a photo
of another.

My Le takes notice.

> MY LE
> Would you be able to take our
> picture?

> GIRL ONE
> Five dong.

> MY LE
> I only have two dong.

> GIRL TWO
> Anything to trade?

My Le pulls up her rucksack and removes the papaya.

> GIRL ONE
> We'll take that...and two dong.

My Le shakes her head and begins to walk away.

                         GIRL TWO
                Okay, okay, the papaya!

My Le stops. She takes a deep breath, kisses Liem on the
forehead.

                         MY LE
                For us.

She slowly hands Girl One the papaya.

Girl Three takes the camera and points it at My Le and Liem.

                         GIRL THREE
                Okay, ready?

My Le adjusts her hair, combs over Liem's hair with her hand,
and stands straight and tall. Both are semi-serious, content.

                         MY LE
                Ready.

Girl three takes the photo, hands My Le the print. She looks
confused.

                         GIRL THREE
                You have to wait for it.

CLOSE IN ON PHOTO - We see My Le and Liem slowly appear.

Satisfied, she stows it in her pack and leaves the store.

EXT. BEACH - AFTERNOON

My Le and Liem sit near the surf. Liem plays and splashes.

Refugee families occupy the beach, some with inner tubes and
flotation devices.

Minh walks up to My Le and Liem.

                         MINH
                I was beginning to think you
                kidnapped my boy.

My Le giggles.

                         MY LE
                I guess I don't want this day to
                end.

Minh sits in the surf next to My Le. They both take in the
moment.

My Le picks up a handful of sand, admires it as if she's
counting each grain.

                    MINH
          It doesn't have to end like this.
          There is a way for you to come with
          us.

                    MY LE
          A way?

Minh stammers a bit before making her an offer.

                    MINH
          We...could marry.

My Le is speechless. Surprised. Baffled.

                    MINH (CONT'D)
          People do it all the time to get
          out of the camps.

                    MY LE
          Oh, no. No, I can't do that. No,
          no. I'm too young and you're still
          married...and we met only a week
          ago...

                    MINH
          I'm a widower now. And you've been
          a mother to my child for a lot
          longer than that. He needs you.

Blind-sided, My Le stands and paces in the sand.

                    MINH (CONT'D)
          It could be a means to an end, My
          Le. A way to reunite you with your
          father.

My Le remains silent. She ponders, looks at Liem, emotion
overwhelms her.

                    MY LE
          I-I can't. Those are all the wrong
          reasons to marry.

                    MINH
          You're a grown woman. How long do
          you want to stay on this island?

She turns and walks away. Half way up the beach, she turns
around. She returns to Minh who is now holding Liem.

                         MY LE
            I will say goodbye at the dock
            tomorrow...if that's okay with you.

                         MINH
            We would like that.

EXT. GALANG CAMP - BOAT DOCK - MORNING

My Le and Minh approach a small but capable boat. My Le
carries Liem down the dock.

REFUGEES gather around the boat as the boarding process
begins. Once aboard, they wave to REFUGEES on shore.

                         MINH
            I'm sorry if I upset you yesterday.
            I was only trying to help.

                         MY LE
            It's okay. I want to thank you for
            thinking of me and my father. It
            was very caring of you. I'm just
            not ready to jump into the unknown
            again.

                         MINH
            I understand.
                (beat)
            You have my information. I will
            write and send pictures. Let's stay
            in touch.

                         MY LE
            Here, I want Liem to have this.
            Something to remember me by.

She hands the Polaroid picture to Minh. He accepts, smiles.

                         MINH
            If you settle in America, look us
            up.

My Le hands Liem to Minh. She kisses them both on the cheek.

                         MY LE
            I will. Have a safe trip.

Minh and Liem board the boat. Once on, they turn and look
back at My Le. Minh grabs Liem's hand and makes him wave.

My Le tears up as the boat pulls away from the dock.

                              FADE OUT:

FADE IN:

INT. PRIMARY/SECONDARY SCHOOL HUT - DAY

SUPER - "SIX MONTHS LATER"

My Le has a picture of a hot dog and displays it in front of
the confused class.

                    MY LE
          In America, the hot dog is a food
          item...not a real dog.

A STUDENT raises his hand. My Le acknowledges.

                    MY LE
          You have a question?

                    STUDENT
          I don't understand. Why do they
          call it that?

Barr sits at the side, giggles a bit then checks his watch.

                    BARR
          Okay, class, that's a great
          question for tomorrow. Right now,
          it's time to go.

The class dismisses. Students EXIT. Barr approaches My Le.

                    BARR
          I have something you might be
          interested in.

He hands My Le a picture. She looks at it, eyes widen.

                    MY LE
          Papa? My papa? You found him?

                    BARR
          We did. One of my UNHCR friends did
          some searching for me...for you.

                    MY LE
          Where is he?

                    BARR
          Arkansas.

                         MY LE
          Ark...?

                         BARR
          Arkansas. He was transferred to
          Fort Smith in the first wave.

She takes a closer look at the photo.

                         MY LE
          But why is he in a wheelchair? Is
          he hurt?

Barr kneels before her, rests a hand on her shoulder.

                         BARR
          He suffered a stroke some time ago.
          His host family is doing a great
          job taking care of him though.

                         MY LE
          When can I see him?

                         BARR
          It's going to take some time to get
          you processed and transferred I'm
          afraid. Could be as long as six
          months or as short as three...with
          a stop or two in-between.

                         MY LE
          A stop?

                         BARR
          Batan, the Philippines, more
          processing there probably. Then
          you'll catch a plane to America.

                         MY LE
          What will it be like for me in
          America?

They EXIT the school.

OUTSIDE SCHOOL

                         BARR
          It won't be easy at first, but you
          have a head start with the
          language. For your fellow
          countryman, it will be a struggle.
          Perhaps you can make that a part of
          your mission in America?

                    MY LE
          What about you?

                    BARR
          I'll stay another six months, head
          back home...then do it all over
          again in another country.

                    MY LE
          You're a kind man, Mr. Barr. You
          have helped our people and we will
          be forever grateful.

                    BARR
          Thank you. I wish I could do
          more...as more needs to be done.

                    BARR (CONT'D)
          You need to head over to
          processing. I told them you'd be in
          after class. Today. Now.

                    MY LE
          I'm leaving soon?

                    BARR
          Probably tomorrow...but you need to
          hustle. Go!

She thanks him again, turns, and sprints away.

My Le runs through the camp...

                                        DISSOLVE TO:

EXT. JUNGLE - MY LE'S DREAM - DAY/NIGHT

My Le running through the jungle. Everything is dream-like,
distorted.

She trips over some brush and falls face first onto the
ground.

A woman's hand reaches down, helps her to her feet.

She is face to face with her mother.

                    LAN
          Don't be long, My Le.

                    MY LE
          Momma...

My Le hears a SOUND behind her and turns. She turns back to her mother and her mother is gone.

She starts to run again.

Through the thickness she struggles, her mother's voice overwhelms her, repeating, ECHOING off the jungle.

In her path, she sees Liem. He sits upright holds his arms out.

She approaches and reaches down and picks him up. There is a tap on her shoulder.

My Le jumps, turns around frightened. The entire crew of the scavenger boat stands before her.

> DRIVER
> Not your child...

She turns and runs further into the woods, trying to scream but unable. The forest morphs into My Tho City.

MY THO CITY - MY LE'S DREAM - CONT'D

She stops in the middle of the street. The firefight consumes everything.

Out of the smoke, she sees her mom and dad walking calmly down the street, holding hands. They smile, untouched by the surrounding fight.

My Le runs toward them but cannot reach them.

> MY LE
> (screaming in Viet)
> Dung ban! Dung ban!

She struggles, unable to make up ground. The street becomes sand. Her feet sink, her pace slows.

AT BEACH - MY LE'S DREAM - CONT'D

She wades out onto a colorless beach.

She approaches the surf and falls to her knees. There is a CLICK. She turns.

Sergeant Hathaway stands with a rifle pointed at her head.

> HATHAWAY
> We call it...war.

                         MY LE
              Dung ban!

ON HIS TRIGGER FINGER - It squeezes. There is a BANG! Then
BLACKNESS.

INT. AIRPLANE - DAY

SUPER - "1980"

                         MY LE
              Dung ban! Dung ban!

My Le is shocked awake by the sound of a BOY SMACKING a toy
at the back of a seat.

She regroups, calms her breathing and averts her attention to
the window. She gazes outside.

MY LE'S POV - ARKANSAS LANDSCAPE - The ground is covered in
snow, an airport runway becomes apparent.

EXT. LITTLE ROCK NATIONAL AIRPORT - TERMINAL - DAY

My Le's plane pulls up to the terminal. We see her face in
the window.

INSIDE TERMINAL

My Le walks into the terminal. Arms crossed, she shivers from
the frigid cold outside. She wears only a light sweater.

An older LADY holds up a sign with My Le's name. She is
Barbara Rice, Cavanaugh church ministry assistant. She's a
mid-sixties fast-talking fireball with energy to spare.

My Le notices and approaches, offers an apprehensive smile.

                         MY LE
              I am My Le Nguyen.

                         BARBARA
                    (deep accent)
              Hi, Miss Noogen. I'm Barbara Rice
              with the Cavanaugh Church. Welcome
              to Arkansas.

My Le continues to shiver.

                         MY LE
              Thank you.

                    BARBARA
          Heavens, you are absolutely frozen.
          Don't you have a winter coat,
          darling?

                    MY LE
                (regards sweater)
          Just this.

                    BARBARA
          Well, we'll just have to get you
          somethin' from one of the shops
          before we go. Come now.

INT. BARBARA'S CAR - DAY

My Le sits in the front seat bundled up in a new winter coat.
She stares at the snow outside as they drive.

                    BARBARA
          You're awful quiet over there,
          darlin'.

                    MY LE
          ...snow?

                    BARBARA
          You're first time seein' snow?
          Well, you can have it. I'm tired of
          it, quite frankly. I'm ready for
          summer.

                    MY LE
          It's very pretty. I want to touch.

                    BARBARA
          You'll have plenty of time to touch
          it when we get to your new home,
          little lady.

                    MY LE
          My father is there?

                    BARBARA
          He is, and boy is he's excited to
          see you again. The whole family is
          excited to meet you. You're gon'
          love 'em.

My Le looks over at Barbara, confused. The delivery too
aggressive, the accent too strong.

                    BARBARA (CONT'D)
          Great people. Been coming to our
          church since forever. And they got
          a boy, too. A bit younger than you,
          but he's a real peach. Just fun to
          be around even though he's a bit
          different with his skin condition
          and all.

                    MY LE
          When did my father arrive?

                    BARBARA
          He was part of the Operation New
          Life program in 1975. Many refugees
          came to Fort Chaffee during that
          year. Wasn't long after that, the
          Catholic Conference found him a
          host family. The Nilson's have been
          taking care of him ever since in
          Fort Smith.

                    MY LE
          Taking care...

                    BARBARA
          Best they can. You'll certainly be
          a big help around the house. The
          stroke left him a bit
          incapacitated.

                    MY LE
          Incap...?

                    BARBARA
          He needs a lot of help. Whole left
          side is paralyzed and he can't talk
          like you or me. Has to write things
          down on his notepad.

My Le resumes her silent gaze out the window.

EXT. NILSON HOUSE - LATE AFTERNOON

Barbara's station wagon pulls into the driveway. The Nilson
house is circa 40's with a small porch.

My Le gets out of the car. Her feet touch snow. She kneels
down and grabs a handful, admires it, then quickly tosses the
cold mass.

The front door opens and the NILSON FAMILY shuffles outside. The wife/mother, ELIZABETH, the fourteen year-old albino son, LUCAS, and the husband/father, MAYNARD.

Lucas, smiling big with sunglasses on, holds a small sign written in crayon that reads, "Welcome, My Le".

> BARBARA
> Hi there, Nilson family! Long trip,
> but we finally made it.

Barbara rushes over to My Le, grabs her by the arm.

> BARBARA (CONT'D)
> Come on, sweetie, let's meet your
> new family.

They great on the porch, but My Le is mostly silent. Her eyes search for her father as she greets the Nilsons.

> BARBARA (CONT'D)
> My Le, this is
> Elizabeth...Lucas...and big daddy,
> Maynard. The Nilsons.

> MAYNARD
> Welcome home, little miss.

> ELIZABETH
> So nice to have you, dear.

Lucas offers a hand. My Le stares momentarily, then accepts.

> ELIZABETH
> So, My Le, there is someone here
> that you're probably dyin' ta'
> meet. Lucas?

> LUCAS
> Be right back!

Lucas runs into the house and returns moments later pushing a wheelchair.

My Le squints to get a look as the wheelchair emerges from the dark interior.

The legs, then the torso, then the face of the MAN in the wheelchair becomes visible.

My Le slowly approaches.

The Nilson's and Barbara watch with eager anticipation.

My Le cups her mouth with her hand, slowly kneels before the
man. His head is cocked a bit sideways, face drooping
slightly. Their eyes meet, an unspoken negative connection.

A tear emerges from My Le. She's in shock.

                    BARBARA
          Praise the Lord. Finally united.
          Dont'cha just love it? Now how
          sweet is that?

                    ELIZABETH
          It's a miracle. Oh, thank you, Lord
          Jesus.

The man begins breathing heavier, becomes agitated, face
twitching, mouth trembling.

My Le moves in closer. Speaks in her native tongue.

                    MY LE
               (subtitled Viet)
          I'm sorry, old man.

She places her hand on his, purses her lip. The sad reality
sets in for both. This is not her father, Nam, but an older
man with the same name and likeness.

                    MY LE (CONT'D)
               (subtitled Viet)
          Someone has made a mistake, haven't
          they? You understand, right?
               (beat)
          I'm not her.

Nam nods his head yes, closes his eyes. Clenches. Exhales.

                    LUCAS
          What did she say?

                    BARBARA
          She's speaking their language,
          Lucas. Lord have mercy, I think I'm
          gonna cry.

                    MAYNARD
          Let's cry inside then. It's too
          damn cold out here.

                    ELIZABETH
          Maynard Robert Nilson, now you
          watch that mouth of yours!

                    BARBARA
          Oh, yes, of course. Y'all get
          yourselves inside where it's warm.
          I've got to get back to the church
          and those two have a lot of
          catching up to do.

Barbara and Elizabeth cheek kiss. Barbara heads to the car.

                    ELIZABETH
          Thank you, darling. We'll see you
          on Sunday!

INT. NILSON HOUSE - MY LE'S ROOM - EARLY EVENING

Elizabeth shows My Le her room.

                    MY LE
          This is more than I can dream of.

                    ELIZABETH
          Dinner in an hour. You must be
          hungry.

                    MY LE
          I am. Thank you, Miss Elizabeth.
          The room is nice.

                    ELIZABETH
          You can just call me Elizabeth or
          Beth. Welcome to your new home.

My Le nods as Elizabeth shuts the door.

My begins to cry. She falls onto the bed, buries her head.

OUTSIDE MY LE'S ROOM

Elizabeth puts her ear to the door. She can hear My Le
crying. She remains momentarily, then walks away.

BACK IN MY LE'S ROOM

My Le lies on her back, holds her family photo up. She stares
at her father in the photo.

She rolls over, looks out the window. The moon's blue note
paints the snowscape.

                    MY LE (V.O. PAST)
          Where are you, papa? Why won't you
          reach out to me?

INT. DINING ROOM - EVENING

At the dinner table: Chicken, mashed potatoes and corn. My Le
tries to look interested.

Lucas, sitting next to My Le, stares at her arm. He reaches
over to touch it.

                    MAYNARD
          What'cha doin' there, boy? Eat up
          now.

                    LUCAS
          She has perfect skin. I wanted to
          touch it.

My Le pulls her arm off the table.

                    ELIZABETH
          Lucas, it's not nice to touch.
          You'll have to excuse him, sweetie.
          He's never seen a young Asian girl
          before.

                    MY LE
          It's okay.

More silence and eating.

                    ELIZABETH
          My Le, we were sorry to hear about
          your brother.

                    MY LE
          My brother?

My Le stops herself, gazes over at Nam. Nam shakes his head.

                    ELIZABETH
          It must have been very difficult
          for you to lose him.

                    MY LE
          Oh, yes, it was. Many people died.
          I miss him.

                    ELIZABETH
          You were not together?

                    MY LE
          We split up, took different boats.
          We lost touch.

She looks over at Nam for confirmation.

                              LUCAS
              I hate my skin.

                              MAYNARD
              Quiet, boy. Your momma has the
              table now.

                              MY LE
              Mr. Nilson, please. I want to know.
              Why does Lucas hate his skin?

She pulls her arm back up onto the table. She presses her arm
against his. He looks to his dad for approval.

                              MAYNARD
              Go on, boy.

                              LUCAS
              Because it makes me feel alone.

                              MY LE
              But you are not alone. You have
              your family. You are a lucky boy.

My Le pats his hand. Comforts him.

                              LUCAS
              I have no friends. Look at me.

                              MY LE
              I am looking at you. Are we not
              friends?
                   (beat)
              Your skin feels just like mine.
              Skin is only a shell, Lucas.
              Underneath, we are all the same.

                              ELIZABETH
              She has a point there, sweetie.

                              MAYNARD
              Damn right. Girl seems wise beyond
              her years. Got that from your
              daddy, right?

Maynard continues to pile food into his mouth.

My Le glances over at Nam, they share a reluctant smile.

INT. NILSON HOUSE - BATHROOM - EVENING

My Le gives Nam a sponge bath.

                              MY LE
                         (subtitled Viet)
                 How many children do you have, Nam?

Nam raises his good hand, displays two fingers.

                           MY LE (CONT'D)
                         (subtitled Viet)
                 I'm an only child. How did I get
                 here?

He points to his writing pad on the counter. My Le reaches
for it and holds it steady for him. He scribbles.

She watches him write.

                           MY LE (CONT'D)
                         (translating, subtitled
                          Viet)
                 I...don't...know. UNHCR
                 mistake...too many people leaving
                 Vietnam...confusion...many names
                 alike.
                         (My LE)
                 What about your family?

He shakes his head, no.

                           MY LE (CONT'D)
                         (subtitled Viet)
                 No? No family? Your children? They
                 are still out there, no?

He continues to shake his head, no.

                           MY LE (CONT'D)
                         (subtitled Viet)
                 But how do you know?

He taps her hand to hold the writing pad. He scribbles.

                           MY LE (CONT'D)
                         (translating, subtitled
                          Viet)
                 Boy...died of deng fever in
                 camp...daughter never found...no
                 trace now...you were last
                 hope...you...you.
                         (My Le)
                 Then we have to let the Nilson's
                 know...

Nam taps her hand frantically, shakes his head no, grunts.

>   MY LE (CONT'D)
>   (subtitled Viet)
>   Why not? She might still be alive.

He taps her hand again to hold the pad. He scribbles.

>   MY LE (CONT'D)
>   (translating, subtitled
>   Viet)
>   They...must...not...know.

He tosses the pencil aside, gives her a firm stare. She nods.

EXT. NILSON HOUSE - DAY

SUPER - "SIX MONTHS LATER"

My Le walks from the mail box with Lucas. He hands her a
letter from the stack.

>   LUCAS
>   For you. Him again.

Excited, she takes it, reads the address. It's from Minh. She
runs inside.

INT. MY LE'S BEDROOM - DAY

My Le opens the envelope. She unfolds a letter, photos drop.

She looks at all of the photos. Various shots of Minh and
Liem in California, palm trees, sunshine, beaches, paradise.

She begins to read the letter, but is interrupted by Maynard
O.S..

>   MAYNARD (O.S.)
>   (shouting)
>   Hey, everyone, come to the living
>   room. Hurry!

IN LIVING ROOM

All are present except Nam. My Le is the last to arrive.

>   MAYNARD
>   Hey, watch this. It's Sixty Minutes
>   and one of the hosts is at a
>   refugee camp.

ON SCREEN - CORRESPONDENT ED BRADLEY pulls refugees out of
the water. He NARRATES the events over the footage. Many

refugees are being rescued from a sinking junk off shore.

                    LUCAS
          Look at all of those people. Is
          that where you were, My Le?

                    MY LE
          This is Pulau Bidong. I was in
          Pulau Galang. They are very close.

                    LUCAS
          I don't think I could live there.

                    MY LE
          You could if you had to.

ON SCREEN - Bradley interviews a Vietnamese woman after
pulling a refugee ashore himself. (ACTUAL EPISODE)

                    BRADLEY
          ...the United States will take all
          (refugees)?

                    WOMAN
          ...yes...

                    BRADLEY
          You really believe that?

                    WOMAN
          ...I hope.

                    LUCAS
          Holy smokes, that's a lot of
          people!

                    MY LE
          There are thousands more you don't
          see.

MY LE'S ROOM

Nam manages the wheelchair through the hallway on his own. He
passes by My Le's room, sees the photos on her bed. Backs up.

Curious, he makes his way clumsily into the room.

He picks up some of the photos, then the letter. He reads it.

                    MINH (V.O.)
          My Le. Thank you for staying in
          touch over the last few months.
                    (MORE)

> MINH (V.O.) (CONT'D)
> Liem is three now, can you believe
> it? He's always running around and
> making messes like little boys do.

EXT. WESTMINSTER, CA - GAS STATION - EVENING

Minh hoses down the gas station island area.

> MINH (V.O. CONT'D)
> I've been working long hours at a
> gas station and saving money.

The OWNER approaches Minh.

> OWNER
> I don't pay you to just hose the
> pad down. Get in the bathroom and
> scrub it.

> MINH (V.O.)
> But the owner is a jerk and I told
> him someday I'll own his station.

He removes his work coveralls and clocks out.

> MINH (V.O. CONT'D)
> California is nice. The sun is
> always out and our area in
> Westminster is growing so fast.
> It's like Little Saigon here.

EXT. BOLSA AVE - NIGHT

Minh walks with his lunch box down the darkened sidewalk.

> MINH (V.O. CONT'D)
> I was sorry to hear that you were
> not able to reunite with your
> father. There seems to be a lot of
> that happening with our people. You
> shouldn't give up hope.

INT. MINH'S APARTMENT - EVENING

He unlocks the door, steps inside. Puts his things down.

> MINH (V.O. CONT'D)
> My brother and his wife own my
> apartment and it's dirt cheap. I
> don't get to see them very often.
> (MORE)

MINH (V.O. CONT'D) (CONT'D)
They live in San Diego now and
rarely come to Orange County.

There is a knock on his door. He opens. His NEIGHBOR, a young
lady with THREE KIDS at her side, hands Liem to Minh.

MINH (V.O. CONT'D)
I've been very fortunate to have a
neighbor who looks after Liem for
me.

He thanks her then shuts the door.

MINH (V.O. CONT'D)
But when I look in his eyes, I see
that he misses you and he misses
his mom.

Minh walks over to the table, retrieves his lunch pail. He
opens it and shares some fruit with Liem.

MINH (V.O. CONT'D)
His favorite picture is the one you
took with him. He looks at it every
day. He calls you maaaaaaaa.

On a small table next to a single chair, the photo is propped
against a lamp. Minh reaches for it. Stares deeply.

MINH (V.O. CONT'D)
Our door is open. It would be
really nice if you could visit
someday.
(beat)
We would like that.

INT. MY LE'S BEDROOM - BACK TO SCENE

My Le steps into the room, shuts the door, startles Nam.

MY LE
I won't bother getting upset. It
was my fault for leaving these out.

She snatches the photos and letter away. Holds them close.

MY LE (CONT'D)
Privacy isn't something I'm used
to, but I do expect it from you.

He points to one of the photos in her clutch. He tries to
mouth the word, "baby."

She pulls the picture up, looks at it.

>   MY LE (CONT'D)
>   Baby? Yes.

He reaches for it. Demands it. Reluctantly, she hands it to
him. He looks at the picture and points to her.

>   MY LE (CONT'D)
>   No, not my baby.

Nam pulls out his pad, wedges it against the chair arm.
Begins scribbling. He holds the pad for her to read.

>   MY LE (CONT'D)
>   Go to him? My home is here now. I
>   want to help.

Nam shakes his head, no. He points at the picture and taps
it. Then taps her arm. He scribbles again.

He shows her the pad. We see the ENGLISH TRANSLATION - "Child
needs mother...I don't!"

>   MY LE (CONT'D)
>   I don't know. I can't just leave.

He scribbles on the pad in Vietnamese. We see the ENGLISH
TRANSLATION - "You rescued? You his mom. Go to him. Go!"

My Le begins to sob.

He writes again, the ENGLISH TRANSLATION - "Don't belong
here."

She sits on the bed, continues to cry. He pulls close. Taps
her knee, then lifts her chin.

He writes again, the ENGLISH TRANSLATION - "Thank you for
help. No future here. Future in California."

>   MY LE (CONT'D)
>   What do I tell the Nilsons?

Nam writes slowly, the ENGLISH TRANSLATION - "The truth."

INT. NILSON HOUSE - KITCHEN - MORNING

Scrambled eggs and bacon for breakfast. Encircling the table,
we see My Le inaudibly explaining her situation to the
Nilsons. As she speaks, a range of emotions capture each of
the Nilsons: happy, sad, concerned, confused, accepting.

                    MY LE (V.O. PRESENT)
          We stretched the truth a bit. Nam
          helped me convince the Nilsons that
          my true purpose was in California
          helping baby Liem. They reluctantly
          agreed.

INT. MINH'S APARTMENT - DAY

Minh carries groceries and mail in one arm, Liem in the
other.

He sets Liem down on the floor, groceries on the table. He
sees My Le's letter and opens it quickly.

He begins reading, a smile forms on his face.

                    MINH
          Well, Liem, it looks as if we're
          going to have a special visitor.

EXT. WESTMINSTER, CA - PHONE BOOTH - DAY

Minh and Liem are stuffed into a phone booth. Minh speaks
inaudibly into the phone. Liem plays with the receiver, makes
BABY NOISES.

                    MINH
          Yes, yes, yes. This is fantastic
          news, My Le. Two weeks is plenty of
          time, take more if you need it.
          Liem is excited too. He won't stop
          grabbing the phone!

EXT. NILSON HOUSE - DAY

Springtime, with blue sky, green grass and wild flowers. My
Le wheels Nam to the edge of the yard, next to the flowers.
She squats next to the wheelchair.

                    MY LE
          Thank you for helping me with the
          plane tickets.

He gives her a thumb's up and nods.

                    MY LE (CONT'D)
          I will come back and visit.
          Promise.

He writes on the pad, shows her.

                         MY LE (CONT'D)
          Of course, I will bring them too.

He writes on the pad again, she reads it.

                         MY LE (CONT'D)
          Yes, I will continue to search for
          my father. Dead or alive, I need
          some closure. I need to move on.
                    (points to her heart)
          Here.

He pats her hand. They both look out over the landscape.

                         MY LE (V.O. PRESENT)
          I did keep my promise to return,
          but it was not to my liking. Three
          years later I would fly back...to
          attend Nam's funeral.

EXT. ORANGE COUNTY, CA. - JOHN WAYNE AIRPORT - AFTERNOON

A beautiful sunny day in So Cal. My Le's plane touches down.

INT. MINH'S CAR - LATER

Minh drives out of the airport terminal. They're all packed
in the front seat of his beat up Toyota. Lots of
conversation. Everyone's in a happy place.

                         MINH
          Orange County is booming right now.
          So many Vietnamese arriving every
          day and businesses going up in
          Westminster, it's crazy. You're
          going to feel right at home here.

                         MY LE
          So sunny and warm, I feel better
          already. I want to see the
          ocean...touch the sand. Will you
          take us?

                         MINH
          Right now? Don't you want to see
          your home first?

My Le pinches Liem's cheek, cuddles with him.

                         MY LE
          I want to go to the beach
          first...with this little man.
                    (MORE)

                    MY LE (CONT'D)
          You're so big now! Oh, I missed
          you, Liem. I missed you so much.
          Okay, I missed you, too, daddy.

EXT. HUNTINGTON BEACH, CA - SUNSET

My Le, Minh and Liem play on the beach. We INTERCUT between
her past with her family and present with Minh and Liem.

                    MY LE (V.O. PRESENT CONT'D)
          The beach was everything I dreamed
          it would be, and California's
          climate was more to my liking. But
          I couldn't help think about my
          father. My memories of him were
          much like this very moment with
          Minh and Liem.

INT. OFFICE BUILDING - BATHROOM - DAY

My Le scrubs a toilet, washes a mirror, stows her gear.

                    MY LE (V.O. PRESENT CONT'D)
          I promised myself I'd never give up
          my search, but at the same time, I
          had to be realistic. I had a new
          life in front of me and it would
          unfold quickly. It was time to go
          to work....

INT. COMMUNITY COLLEGE - DAY

My Le sits in a class and studies.

                    MY LE (V.O. PRESENT CONT'D)
          Time to go to school...

INT. ST. ANSELM'S IMMIGRANT AND REFUGEE C.C. - DAY

My Le stands before a small class of REFUGEES. A hand is
raised, question asked. She answers inaudibly.

                    MY LE (V.O. PRESENT CONT'D)
          Time to give back. I was now the
          papaya.

                                        FADE OUT:

FADE IN:

INT. GROCERY STORE - DAY

SUPER - "TEN YEARS LATER"

My Le stands in line with a cart full of charity food. There
is another Vietnamese WOMAN in front of her, and an impatient
CAUCASIAN COUPLE behind her.

>   MAN
>   Ridiculous. They're taking over, I
>   swear. Never had to wait in line
>   here.

>   WOMAN
>   Shhh...don't talk too loud.

>   MAN
>   Oh hooey! Gook's can't understand
>   what I'm saying anyway. They have
>   their own stores down on Bolsa, why
>   don't they go there?

My Le steps aside and gestures for the couple to go ahead of
her.

>   MY LE
>   (articulate)
>   I understand you're in a hurry,
>   sir. Would you like to go in front
>   of me?

The woman smacks her husband on the shoulder.

>   WOMAN
>   Can't understand, huh? You big
>   bully.
>   (to My Le)
>   No, we'll wait our turn honey.

INT. ST. ANSELM'S IMMIGRANT AND REFUGEE C.C. - DAY

My Le pushes a cart of food into the center. The community
director, CHARLES NGUYEN, accepts the cart.

>   CHARLES
>   Thank you for picking this food up
>   for us, Nancy. No issues?

>   MY LE
>   Oh, the usual. You know how it is
>   out there in the trenches.

                              CHARLES
                    Unfortunately the big chain stores
                    are the most charitable. Will you
                    be teaching here tomorrow?

                              MY LE
                    No, studying. Two more days of it.
                    I've asked Myra to fill in for me.

                              CHARLES
                    Cal Fullerton, right? Your
                    master's?

                              MY LE
                    If my head doesn't explode first!
                        (beat)
                    So Charles, was there any progress
                    on my father?

                              CHARLES
                    We're still trying. This is really
                    messy right now and the paper
                    trails are spotty at best. There
                    are fewer refugees making it in
                    now, and many are being repatriated
                    to Vietnam from the various camps
                    around the world.

                              MY LE
                    I want to help though, I really do.

                              CHARLES
                    Your are helping. Trust me. And we
                    are doing everything we can to help
                    you. This process will take time
                    I'm afraid.

INT. MINH AND MY LE'S HOUSE - EVENING

My Le walks into the house. It's empty.

She walks into the kitchen and sees a vase full of roses and
a card from Minh.

                              MINH (V.O.)
                    Eight years, my love. What can I
                    say? A miracle brought us together,
                    but it will be our love for each
                    other that keeps the torch lit.

FLASHBACK - WEDDING DAY - JUSTICE OF THE PEACE

They finish their vows, rings are fitted, kisses made.

                         MINH (V.O. CONT'D)
                    I will forever remember the day we
                    said our vows.

They walk to the counter to sign.

                         JUDGE
                    You may sign here, ma'am and your
                    husband here. Will you be using
                    your English names?

                         MY LE
                    We don't have English names.

                         JUDGE
                    You can chose one for the marriage
                    certificate if you like.

My Le looks up on the wall, sees portraits of Ronald and
Nancy Reagan.

                         MY LE
                    Nancy. I like that name.

                         MINH (V.O. CONT'D)
                    And the look on my face when you
                    chose Nancy as your English name.

Minh look up at the portraits. Shakes his head.

                         JUDGE
                    Sir? How about you?

                         MINH
                    No, just Minh. Thank you.

BACK TO SCENE - MINH AND MY LE'S HOUSE

                         MINH (V.O. CONT'D)
                    Liem and I are both lucky to have
                    you. Good luck with finals this
                    week. I'm taking Liem fishing for a
                    couple of days so you can study.

She puts the card down, admires their family portrait.

EXT. CAL FULLERTON CAMPUS - COMMENCEMENT - DAY

Nancy Nguyen is called, My Le enters the stage, shakes hands
with the presiding officer, accepts her scroll tube. She
walks across stage. She looks a bit empty, expressionless.

Minh and Liem are in the audience. They clap.

                    LIEM
          Why isn't she smiling, papa? I
          would be jumping up and down if I
          got my master's degree.

                    MINH
          I know why.

                    LIEM
          Why?

                    MINH
          I will let her tell you.

INT. CAR - DAY

Minh drives. My Le is quiet. Liem is concerned.

                    LIEM
          We're very proud of you, mom.
               (beat)
          Mom? You okay?

                    MY LE
          I'm okay.

                    LIEM
          You don't look okay.

My Le glances over at Minh. Minh remains eyes forward,
silent.

                    MY LE
          I'll be fine. I have a lot on my
          mind.

                    LIEM
          Papa, I tried.

                    MINH
          Talk to him, please. I told him you
          would.

                    MY LE
               (beat)
          I'm an only child, Liem, like you.
          Your father and I have been trying
          to give you siblings, to build our
          family.

INT. MINH AND MY LE'S HOUSE - DAY

Minh comforts My Le on the sofa. She sobs.

                    MY LE (CONT'D)(V.O.)
          But it's not going to happen. We
          got news from the doctor yesterday
          that I could not have children.

BACK IN CAR

                    MY LE (CONT'D)
          I carry a family curse, like my
          parents.

                    LIEM
          It's okay. It sounds like God has a
          different plan for us. Right, papa?

                    MINH
          That's right. We have a house, we
          own two gas stations, your mom got
          her master's degree in education,
          she volunteers and helps the
          refugees coming in and...you're a
          good student. That's a pretty good
          plan, wouldn't you say mom?
                    (subtitled Vietnamese)
          It's no disgrace to move out of the
          way of the elephant.

                    MY LE (V.O.)
          I could always count on Minh to see
          the bright side.

INT. SCHOOL - MORNING

My Le stands before a class of junior high students. Liem is
in the class.

                    MY LE (V.O. PRESENT)
          I would spend the next ten years
          teaching. I even had Liem as a
          student for one year before he
          moved on to high school.

EXT. GAS STATION - DAY

Minh approaches Liem, now one of the attendants.

                    MY LE (V.O. PRESENT)
          We now had four gas stations and we
          were living comfortably. Liem was
          learning the business quickly.

Minh walks to the back of the station. There is a freight
carrier picking up a load of boxes.

                    MY LE (V.O. PRESENT)
          We wanted to be more charitable, so
          we used the stations as a staging
          area for goods to be shipped to the
          needy in Vietnam.

The freight DRIVER hands Minh a form to fill out. Shrugs his
shoulders.

Minh refuses to fill out the form, hands it back to the
driver.

                    MY LE (V.O. PRESENT)
          But that didn't last long, as U.S.
          Customs got wind of what we were
          doing and put a stop to it.

Minh points to Liem and has him unload the truck.

EXT. ORANGE COUNTY CHAMBER OF COMMERCE - DAY

My Le walks past the chamber sign and into the building.

INT. ORANGE COUNTY CHAMBER OF COMMERCE - NANCY'S OFFICE

At her desk, sitting tall. She shuffles through her mail.

                    MY LE (V.O. PRESENT)
          I sat on the board for the Orange
          County chamber of commerce for
          several years. I would eventually
          become president and CEO. It was
          then that I decided to retire from
          teaching and spend more time at
          home...more time searching...

One of the envelopes has a big, red TED logo on it. She opens
it.

INT. MIN AND MY LE'S HOUSE - DINNER - EVENING

Liem is eating hastily and reading My Le's TED letter at the
dinner table.

                         LIEM
            Yeah, TED is huge. A real honor to
            be selected. You need to do it.

                         MINH
            Did you apply for this?

                         MY LE
            No, the city of Orange petitioned
            for me to be a TED speaker. I don't
            even know what I'd talk about.

                         MINH
            How about twenty-one years of
            struggle?

                         LIEM
            Do it, mom.

Liem shovels more food into his mouth.

                         MY LE
            See what having two jobs does to
            you? You never taste your food
            anymore.

                         LIEM
            We talked about this. I'm paying
            for grad school on my own.

                         MINH
            Stubborn, like someone else I know.

                         LIEM
            Not stubborn. Grateful. I'm not
            going to be a burden to you guys.

                         MY LE
            You will never be a burden to us.
            Ever. You understand me?

                         LIEM
            Yes, ma'am.

                         MY LE
            Good, now you should just quit the
            second job, keep your job at the
            station. You have flexibility there
            and decent pay.

                         LIEM
            I need the second job. Really.
            Just...trust me on this, please.

                              MY LE
                    Second job, second job. We don't
                    even know what you're doing at the
                    second job. What is it?

Liem shovels in a last bite, stands up.

                              LIEM
                    Oh, wow, look at that. I'm running
                    late. I really need to go now.
                    Please excuse me?

                              MINH
                    No! Not until you thank your mom.

Liem stands, walks over to My Le. Plants a kiss on her cheek.

                              LIEM
                    Do the TED talk, mom. Do it for the
                    Boat People.

                              MY LE
                    I'll think about it. Go on, get out
                    of here! Shoo!

Liem runs out of the room.

                              MINH
                    When?

                              MY LE
                    When...what?

                              MINH
                    When is this TED thing?

                              MY LE
                    Four weeks.

                              MINH
                    Liem's right. You need to do it.

                                        FADE OUT:

FADE IN:

INT. UC IRVINE AUDITORIUM - TED EVENT

The auditorium is fixated on My Le. Many are wiping away
tears. There is utter silence, except for My Le.

                              MY LE
                    History tried to crush us...but we
                    endured.
                              (MORE)

                    MY LE (CONT'D)
          There is living proof all around
          you...in your community...in this
          audience. These harrowing journeys
          brought us to you, and we are ever
          so grateful for the opportunities
          provided to us, the Boat People.
          Although I was unable to locate my
          father, I think I'm finally at
          peace with his...

A man stands up, center audience, and walks down the stairs
toward the stage. It's Liem. My Le is interrupted by the
stir.

                    MY LE (CONT'D)
          ...I'm at peace...Liem?

Liem approaches the stage, TWO SECURITY PERSONNEL try to stop
him. He holds up his hands, continues to approach. Rustling
from the audience.

                    LIEM
          It's okay, I'm her son.

                    SECURITY ONE
          You have to remain seated, sir.

                    MY LE
          Liem, you can't come up here.

                    LIEM
          I need to come up there. I need to
          say something. Please.

TED event coordinator, Sharon Vu, enters the stage with a
microphone. She asks the security personnel to allow him to
come up to the stage.

                    SHARON
          It's okay, son. Come on up. We're
          running long, you only have a
          moment. My Le, do you mind?

She looks around the room, at Liem, at Sharon, tries to grasp
the situation.

                    MY LE
          It's okay. Let him speak.

He grabs the microphone, takes a deep breath.

                    LIEM
          I'm sorry, mom. You won't be able
          to finish this without me.
                    (MORE)

                         LIEM (CONT'D)
                    (beat)
              Thank you, everyone. I do apologize
              for the interruption, I'll try to
              be brief. I am Liem Le Nguyen, and
              this woman is the reason I'm
              standing here tonight. You know the
              story now, you know how she made
              sure I, and many like me, had a
              fighting chance. How do you thank
              someone like that? How? I thought
              long and hard and realized that I
              couldn't thank her...without lying
              to her.
                    (audience stirs)
              Yeah, I know, crazy. Anyway, I've
              never lied to her, ever, but I had
              no problem with it
              this...one...time. So, I want to
              confess. I hope you can forgive me.
                    (to her)
              I'm sorry, mom. That second job I
              told you about? There was no second
              job.

My Le is looks confused. Some audience reaction.

                         LIEM (CONT'D)
              You see, for the last six months,
              I've been out...searching. It
              wasn't easy and I almost gave up
              several times. But you know what? A
              power above gave me a lucky
              break...all the pieces came
              together, and I found _who_ I was
              looking for. I found _him_...for you.
              Your father.

My Le's mouth is agape. She's breathless, frozen. She inches
toward Liem. His eyes fill with water.

More audience reaction.

                         MY LE
                    (choked up)
              But Liem, How?...Where?

Liem grabs her by the shoulders, looks deep in her eyes.

                         LIEM
              Turn around.

He helps her turn. She sees her father ENTER the stage. The
audience gasps.

                    MY LE
                (breaking down)
            Oh my god, papa...

Nam, in his mid-60's now, walks slowly toward her.

Liem helps My Le across the stage. Me Le breaks away and
gives her father a long, warm hug.

The audience erupts. Much clapping, celebration.

                    MY LE (CONT'D)
            Oh, papa. Papa I missed you so!
            much!

                    NAM
            My baby girl.

                    MY LE
            I knew you were out there, I just
            knew it...and I never gave up hope.

                    NAM
            I know now how much you tried. I'm
            so sorry, My Le.

Liem watches the exchange. My Le pulls him over.

                    MY LE
            Come here you little shit.

She gives him a big hug.

                    MY LE (CONT'D)
            I spent my whole life looking for
            this man. Where did you find him?.

Liem looks to Nam for approval. Nam nods.

                    LIEM
            Vietnam.

                    MY LE
            What?

                    NAM
            I never left.

                    MY LE
            I was looking in the wrong
            direction the whole time?

INT. TRAN HOUSE - FLASHBACK

Mrs. Tran and Anh look out the window, they see My Le standing at the front door.

Anh turns to Nam and Mr. Tran, looking for instruction.

                    ANH
          She's here, just like you said.

                    NAM
          But I'm not. You must not tell her
          I'm in the other room.

                    MR. TRAN
          Are you sure about this my friend?

                    NAM
          I'm sure. She can't risk being seen
          with me. Hand her this
          letter...then send her on her way.

                    MRS. TRAN
          What is the letter?

                    NAM
          A distraction.

Nam disappears around the corner.

The Trans sits quietly in the living room.

My Le continues to KNOCK on the door.

MR. TRAN gestures for Anh, his daughter, to answer.

Anh opens the door. There stands My Le, dirty, tired.

                    ANH
          My Le!

Anh and Mrs. Tran greet her at the door.

MRS. TRAN pulls My Le into the house like a worried mother.

                    MRS. TRAN
          Oh, my! My Le, you're ragged. Anh,
          make a spot for My Le.

                    MR. TRAN
          She can have my spot.

They escort her in and set her down on Mr. Tran's favorite chair.

IN SPARE ROOM - AROUND THE CORNER

Nam listens in as the Tran's help My Le. He can hear her
reading the letter, eating dinner, asking for money, then her
departure as the front door shuts.

He pulls a cigarette out, lights it. On his face, sadness,
loss, regret.

Mr. Tran walks into the room.

> MR. TRAN
> I hope you know what you just did
> to that young lady.

There is a long pause, he inhales, holds it, then exhales.

> NAM
> I just saved her life.

BACK TO PRESENT - UC IRVINE AUDITORIUM

Sharon walks over and taps them on the shoulders.

> SHARON
> We need to wrap this up, folks.

> NAM
> I will tell you everything at home.

> MY LE
> No, I have a better place.

My Le grabs her father and Liem and turns to the audience.
The audience continues to clap.

EXT. HUNTINGTON BEACH - SUNSET

My Le, Nam, Minh and Liem walk down the beach. It's golden
hour, the sun drops into the horizon.

> MY LE
> You were within my grasp...a room
> away from me that day.

> NAM
> It was the hardest decision of my
> life, and it was the only way to
> keep you alive.

> MINH
> Your military profile must have
> been a terrible burden.

                    NAM
          It did me no favors. I was
          eventually captured, sent to a
          reeducation camp for four years,
          tortured, and nearly killed. Had
          you stayed with me My Le, you would
          have suffered a fate worse than
          mine.

They stop and look out over the surf, into the setting sun.

                    LIEM
          We're all lucky to be alive, I
          guess.

                    MY LE
          It's not luck, Liem. We chose to be
          the papaya. Right papa?

Nam affirms, smiling.

                                        FADE OUT:

                    The End

Made in the USA
Columbia, SC
05 December 2017